Vocabulary Workout for the SAT/ACT

Volume 4

Vocabulary Workout for the SAT/ACT

Volume 4

Justin Grosslight

Published by JJMG Enterprises LLC

JJMG Enterprises LLC
30 N. Gould St.
Suite N
Sheridan, WY 82801
USA

Editorial:
Justin Grosslight, head author and editor.

ISBN: 978-0-9984841-4-3

10 9 8 7 6 5 4 3 2 1

Preface

Becoming an expert in any language is hard work. Regardless of whether English is your mother tongue, more advanced reading and vocabulary skills often accrue slowly and only with a sustained commitment. Because of this, transitioning from communicating in popular English to becoming a consumer of scholarly and intellectual prose can be an arduous journey. While there is no supplement for reading erudite materials, building a vocabulary and an understanding of intellectual concepts is critical for language mastery.

In writing the *Vocabulary Workout* series, I had in mind the myriad individuals who are fluent in conversational English but who want to take their writing skills and vocabulary to the next level. Many of today's students and professionals seek to build these skills, but find the task extraneous to their immediate needs, overly pedantic, or dreadfully time consuming. The *Vocabulary Workout* series aims to ease that process. Unlike other vocabulary books, many of which are merely extended lists, ours are replete with exercises; there are also lessons to help you understand the roots of words and intellectual terms. And the words are useful: they have been gleaned from statistical examination of dozens of SAT® and ACT® college entrance exams, which in turn excerpt their readings from a wide array of sophisticated prose materials.

This is the final volume in a four-volume series. A complete edition that combines all four of volumes of this series is also available. The words in these books are suitable for either classroom study or independent preparation. Do note, however, that these words do not constitute an exhaustive vocabulary list necessary for success.

Writing these books has been an evolving process, and I have enjoyed receiving feedback as it develops. In particular, I would like to thank Vu Le, Antonio Madrid, Uyen Nguyen, and especially Yannick Lalonde for their contributions, sustained support, and constructive criticism. Several students – Helen Dang, Duc Doan, Julian Ho, Quoc Huynh, Phong Le, Alice Nguyen, Nguyen Nguyen, and Hannah Truong – have gladly provided input and frank suggestions as they used drafts of this book to prepare for their SAT® examinations. I also would like to thank Dr. Clive Keevil for allowing pilot versions of these lessons to be taught at the Australian International School (AIS) in Ho Chi Minh City. Last but not least, I would like to thank Robert Fouldes and Huong Nguyen for their cover design upon the book's completion.

I hope that this book will be as immensely useful to you as it has been for the students who used it in its gestation period. With that said, good luck on your vocabulary endeavors!

Justin Grosslight

How to Use This Book

As was the case in our previous three volumes, this book is intended to help build your vocabulary; it is a strategically organized catalogue of 250 words that appear in intellectual and scholarly English, especially in college and university entrance examinations. It is not, however, intended to be your sole source of learning words. Ideally, this book should be used in tandem with reading other scholarly and intellectual materials to help nurture your vocabulary growth.

Often to fully understand a word and its meaning(s), it is helpful to see a word used in context many times. To reinforce this idea, the exercises contained in this book often require dictionary use. By looking up words in a dictionary, you can read samples of their uses in various settings and then apply what you have learned to the exercises in this text. Doing so will provide an active approach to building an extensive vocabulary. This book's exercises also use a consistent intellectual vocabulary to complement the focal words of each lesson. Learning these words should further enhance your verbal skills.

At a stable pace, one should be able to absorb approximately fifty words, or ten lessons, per week. We have provided review quizzes after every ten lessons to help facilitate your study. One can study more words, of course, but diminishing returns may occur if more than twenty lessons are absorbed each week. Ideally this book should be studied at a moderate pace consistently over a long duration, allowing for time to let words sink in slowly. There are also many reasons why someone should use this book: whether you want to build a more solid vocabulary, you want to prepare for an examination, or you simply hope to sound erudite, all are good reasons for using this text. Whatever your purpose of study, however, it is imperative that you never cease to explore new vocabularies.

Possessing a solid vocabulary can help you enter a strong academic program, can make you more attractive for a corporate job, and can make you sound more articulate and knowledgeable. I hope you enjoy the fourth leg of your quest to broaden your vocabulary with this book.

TABLE OF CONTENTS

Lesson 171 .... **1**

Word Search: Lessons 171-180 11

Vocabulary Review: Lessons 171-180 12

A Crowd of "ISMs": A-L 13

Lesson 181 .... **15**

Crossword Puzzle: Lessons 181-190 25

Vocabulary Review: Lessons 181-190 26

A Crowd of "ISMs": M-Z 27

Lesson 191 .... **29**

Word Search: Lessons 191-200 39

Vocabulary Review: Lessons 191-200 40

Long Live Latin! 41

Idiomatic Expressions I 43

Lesson 201 .... **48**

Crossword Puzzle: Lessons 201-210 58

Vocabulary Review: Lessons 201-210 59

Idiomatic Expressions II 60

Lesson 211 .... **65**

Word Search: Lessons 211-220 75

Vocabulary Review: Lessons 211-220 76

Idiomatic Expressions III 77

Key Words With Multiple Definitions 81

Answer Key **84**

Glossary **94**

Lesson 171

NEW WORDS

veiled
vāld

manifest
ˈmanəˌfest

dismantle
disˈmantl

flourish
ˈfləriSH

oracle
ˈôrəkəl

PROPHECIES REVEALED

Roland had recently been feeling lost and despondent. Hoping to find some direction and happiness in his life, he decided to visit someone who claimed to be an **oracle** that could see what one's future holds. When Roland arrived at the home of the self-proclaimed prophet, the oracle was sitting in a dimly lit room with his face **veiled** underneath a sheer cloth. With a **flourish,** the oracle made a gesture at Roland to take a seat. After listening to Roland's troubles, the oracle advised Roland that in order to find his inner path he must **dismantle** his preconceived notion of what happiness is. Only then, when he looked inside himself and understood what it meant for him to be "happy," would the truth **manifest** itself so Roland could follow a meaningful path in life.

Definitions: Try matching the words in the list with the appropriate definitions. If you are stuck, check the glossary in the back of the book or the passage at the top of the page.

1. veiled __________ a. (n.) 1.a bold or extravagant gesture; 2. an ornamental flowing curve in writing; (v.) to grow or develop in a healthy or vigorous way
2. manifest __________ b. to take something apart
3. dismantle __________ c. covered or concealed
4. flourish __________ d. a person with great wisdom; someone believed to communicate with a deity
5. oracle __________ e. (n.) a customs document listing the people and contents of a ship, train, or plane; (v.) 1. to show or demonstrate clearly; 2. to be evidence of, to prove; 3. (of a ghost or an illness) to appear

Sentences: Try to use the words above in a sentence below. Remember that a word ending may be changed or its figure of speech slightly altered.

6. Bri felt that she had the flu as early symptoms began to ____________________.
7. If you want your garden to ____________________, you must make sure the plants receive plentiful water and sunlight.
8. Many people turned to the ____________________ in times of need, hoping that he could give them a divine answer to their problems.
9. Larry looked at his enemy with thinly ____________________ contempt.
10. Dylan ____________________ his computer in an attempt to diagnose the issues he was having with it.

Lesson 172

PIRATE THREAT

Back in the sixteenth century, the town of Cabral constantly feared **predation** by pirates. Citizens of the town saw the pirates sporadically, as they were **itinerant** on the high seas. But when they came to town, they were **pugnacious** and robbed everyone of their cherished and expensive goods. Often the pirates were so terrifying as to harm people. Though citizens begged for **clemency**, the pirates usually attacked them and robbed them blind. In the event someone was neither assaulted nor robbed, the case was surely deemed **anomalous**, and that person was deemed to be very lucky. Only after Cabral received more advanced weaponry in the following century was it able to ward off its seafaring enemies.

NEW WORDS

clemency
ˈklemənsē

predation
priˈdāSHən

anomalous
əˈnämələs

pugnacious
pəgˈnāSHəs

itinerant
īˈtinərənt, iˈtin-

Definitions: Try matching the words in the list with the appropriate definitions. If you are stuck, check the glossary in the back of the book or the passage at the top of the page.

1.	clemency	________	a.	eager or quick to argue or fight
2.	predation	________	b.	deviating from what is normal or expected
3.	anomalous	________	c.	traveling from place to place
4.	pugnacious	________	d.	lenience or mercy
5.	itinerant	________	e.	the act of preying on other animals; attacking or plundering

Sentences: Try to use the words above in a sentence below. Remember that a word ending may be changed or its figure of speech slightly altered.

6. The ____________________ results of the experiment baffled scientists.
7. Due to his ____________________ nature, you never knew where in the world Gus might be at any given time of the year.
8. Ralph's____________________ personality made it difficult for him to make close friends.
9. Joshua's parents granted little ____________________ in punishing him for not doing his homework: they scolded him at length and forced him to study more.
10. The spines on a porcupine's back are an effective defense against ____________________.

Lesson 173

NEW WORDS

aroma
əˈrōmə

brusque
brəsk

imposter
imˈpästər

renew
riˈn(y)o͞o

intermittent
ˌintərˈmitnt

A NICE CHIANTI

As a wine connoisseur, Jordan made sure to attend the **intermittent** wine festivals in his city whenever they were held. He had a liking for wine that probably stemmed from being raised by parents that made and bottled their own wine. Each time he went to the local wine festival, it would remind him of his childhood years and **renew** his love for the fermented beverage. Unfortunately, some of the dishonest wine-sellers at these festivals spoke to him in a **brusque** manner, trying to sell him lower quality, **imposter** wines. They, however, were never able to fool Jordan, who was an expert at identifying authentic wines by their unique **aromas**.

Definitions: Try matching the words in the list with the appropriate definitions. If you are stuck, check the glossary in the back of the book or the passage at the top of the page.

1.	aroma	________	a.	occurring at irregular intervals
2.	brusque	________	b.	a distinctive, pleasant smell
3.	imposter	________	c.	offhand or abrupt in speech or manner
4.	renew	________	d.	a person who deceives others by pretending to be someone else
5.	intermittent	________	e.	to make new, fresh, or strong again

Sentences: Try to use the words above in a sentence below. Remember that a word ending may be changed or its figure of speech slightly altered.

6. Matthew's ____________________ comments on the speech came as a surprise to everyone because he usually is reserved and thinks things through before he talks.
7. The ____________________ rests that Michelle needed to take during her morning run indicated to her that she needed to exercise more regularly.
8. Stewart claimed to be an experienced pilot, but he turned out to be a(n) ____________________ who had never stepped foot in a cockpit.
9. The depressed man decided to go on a meditation retreat to see if he could ____________________ his sense of purpose in his life.
10. The satisfying ____________________ of fresh bread brought back memories of when Lisa used to work in a bakery.

Lesson 174

CAPTIVATED BY CALAMITY

Although Martha was an outwardly cheerful and **congenial** person, she had a dark obsession with **catastrophes**. She loved reading newspaper articles about natural disasters, and her favorite novels were those that contained **motifs** of death and destruction. She was particularly fascinated by the Hindenburg disaster, in which the **voluptuous** frame of an airship caught fire as it **hovered** about 100 meters above where it was supposed to land and then crashed to the ground, killing 36 people.

NEW WORDS

motif
mō'tēf

hover
'həvər

congenial
kən'jēnyəl

catastrophe
kə'tastrəfē

voluptuous
və'ləpCHəwəs

Definitions: Try matching the words in the list with the appropriate definitions. If you are stuck, check the glossary in the back of the book or the passage at the top of the page.

1.	motif	__________	a.	to remain in one place in the air
2.	hover	__________	b.	a terrible disaster
3.	congenial	__________	c.	a theme that is repeated through a book, story, etc.; a decorative pattern
4.	catastrophe	__________	d.	suggesting sensual pleasure by fullness and beauty of form
5.	voluptuous	__________	e.	suitable or appropriate; pleasant

Sentences: Try to use the words above in a sentence below. Remember that a word ending may be changed or its figure of speech slightly altered.

6. Wendy's ____________________ crimson dress accentuated her natural beauty.
7. The helicopter ____________________ noisily over the helipad as it prepared to land.
8. The residents of the coastal town prepared for a(n) ____________________ after hearing the news that a hurricane might pass in its vicinity.
9. Abnormal distortions in mundane objects are a recurring ____________________ in the artist's works.
10. The quality that Anthony liked most about Winona was her ____________________ personality, which made her easy to talk to.

Lesson 175

NEW WORDS

autocrat
'ôtə͵krat

debris
də'brē, ͵dā-

debacle
di'bakəl, -'bäkəl

delusion
di'lo͞oZHən

recluse
'rek͵lo͞os, ri'klo͞os, 'rek͵lo͞oz

A MISUSE OF POWER

Everybody in the office loathed Dwight, the assistant regional manager at the paper company. Whenever the **reclusive** manager was away, which was often, Dwight became the stand-in boss, though his coworkers thought he acted more like an **autocrat**. He seemed to be under the **delusion** that he had complete control over the workings of the office and was immune to the general etiquette that governed acceptable work behavior. He had a short temper and became quickly enraged when people did not follow his directions exactly. One day, in a short fit of rage, Dwight kicked over a desk in the office, covering the room with **debris**. Luckily for Dwight's coworkers, once the manager found out about the **debacle**, he demoted Dwight to a position with less power, as Dwight could clearly not handle this level of responsibly.

Definitions: Try matching the words in the list with the appropriate definitions. If you are stuck, check the glossary in the back of the book or the passage at the top of the page.

1.	autocrat	__________	a.	a complete failure
2.	debris	__________	b.	scattered fragments
3.	debacle	__________	c.	one who lives a solitary existence and who often avoids people
4.	delusion	__________	d.	a ruler who has absolute power
5.	recluse	__________	e.	a belief that is not true; a false idea

Sentences: Try to use the words above in a sentence below. Remember that a word ending may be changed or its figure of speech slightly altered.

6. Frank knew it was probably a(n) ______________________, but he constantly had the feeling that he was being watched.
7. After the ______________________ that was his first musical, Hugh had difficulty finding a theater that would show his new performance piece.
8. Phil's boss acted like a(n) ______________________ and always ignored any input from his employees.
9. Though he was once very sociable, Phillip became something of a(n) ______________________ after his mother's death: he spoke to few people and was no longer much involved in anything.
10. It will take weeks to clean up all of the ______________________ that the earthquake created.

Lesson 176

MELANCHOLY MITCH

Mitch used to be a happy and energetic man, but ever since the death of his wife he had become **lugubrious**. He was so downtrodden that his friends saw him as the **incarnation** of sadness itself. They no longer enjoyed spending time with him because he would become very **querulous** and argumentative when they were around him. His friends **postulated** that this meant that he did not want to be around them, but this isolation only made Mitch's sorrow grow worse. Mitch finally decided to visit a psychiatrist, who prescribed him antidepressants to combat his depressive symptoms. After a few weeks of taking the medication, Mitch's friends noticed some **salutary** effects in his demeanor, although the depression still had not fully gone away.

NEW WORDS

querulous
ˈkwer(y)ələs

postulate
ˈpäsCHələt (n.) ˈpäsCHəˌlāt (v.)

lugubrious
ləˈg(y)o͞obrēəs

salutary
ˈsalyəˌterē

incarnation
ˌinkärˈnāSHən

Definitions: Try matching the words in the list with the appropriate definitions. If you are stuck, check the glossary in the back of the book or the passage at the top of the page.

1.	querulous	__________	a.	full of sadness or sorrow
2.	postulate	__________	b.	a person who represents a quality or idea
3.	lugubrious	__________	c.	complaining in an annoyed way
4.	salutary	__________	d.	(n.) a thing assumed to be true as the basis for reasoning; (v.) to assume the truth or basis of something for the basis of reasoning or belief
5.	incarnation	__________	e.	having a good or helpful result (especially after something unpleasant has happened)

Sentences: Try to use the words above in a sentence below. Remember that a word ending may be changed or its figure of speech slightly altered.

6. Many people believe that the serial killer was the ____________________ of evil itself.
7. Susan ____________________ that it would be difficult to have a discussion about Judaism without first accepting that there is a unique, Jewish God.
8. The car accident was tragic but served as a(n) ____________________ reminder to be more careful on the road.
9. Betsy's eight-year-old son became insufferably ____________________ whenever he didn't get what he wanted.
10. Nick tried to hide his depression from his friends, but they knew something was wrong by the sound of his ____________________ voice.

NEW WORDS

antipathy
an'tipəTHē

durable
'd(y)o͝orəbəl

gratuitous
grə't(y)o͞oitəs

euphoria
yo͞o'fôrēə

perennial
pə'renēəl

Lesson 177

BIPOLAR BEAUTY

Kay's bipolar disorder was both a source of **perennial** distress as well as endless inspiration. As an artist, Kay used both the positive and negative aspects of her disorder to create her works. The intense moments of **euphoria** she felt periodically sent her on a frenzied high that aroused within her a passionate desire to express these powerful emotions. On the other hand, art gave Kay an outlet to work out the **antipathy** and **gratuitous** anger she felt during her low periods. There was a sharp contrast in her work between the pieces she created during her highs and those made during her lows, but Kay believed that all of her works as a whole were a depiction of the volatile yet **durable** spirit that defined her life.

Definitions: Try matching the words in the list with the appropriate definitions. If you are stuck, check the glossary in the back of the book or the passage at the top of the page.

1.	antipathy	________	a.	able to withstand wear, pressure or damage
2.	durable	________	b.	intense happiness and excitement
3.	gratuitous	________	c.	1. existing or continuing in the same way for a long time; 2. (of people) appearing permanently engaged in a specified way of life; 3. (of plants) living for several years
4.	euphoria	________	d.	not necessary or appropriate
5.	perennial	________	e.	a strong feeling of dislike

Sentences: Try to use the words above in a sentence below. Remember that a word ending may be changed or its figure of speech slightly altered.

6. Evan has had countless joyous moments in his life, but nothing could surpass the ____________________ he felt when he first fell in love.
7. It is better to buy something expensive and ____________________ rather than something cheap and easily breakable.
8. The lack of manners that many children display was the main factor contributing to David's ____________________ for little kids.
9. Theresa refused to buy the video game for her son because of the ____________________ violence that it contained.
10. A(n) ____________________ problem of the struggling artist was the difficulty in keeping her original inspiration alive.

Lesson 178

REGGIE'S REVENGE

Reggie was a dynamic, **kinetic** boy. He liked to ride his bicycle around town, but the bullies at the school made this difficult to do. They made fun of him and the **hovel** he lived in and regularly deflated the air in Reggie's bike tires, thus **hampering** Reggie's curiosity for exploration. Feeling sad about his son's plight, Reggie's father advised him that in order to stop the bullies from bothering him, Reggie would have to stand up for himself. Although he had some **misgivings** about his father's advice, Reggie decided to follow it. The next day, when someone tried to let the air out of Reggie's bike tires, Reggie became the **embodiment** of fury and unleashed his deep-seated rage on his tormentor. His retaliation sent the bully to the nurse's office and also sent Reggie to detention, but it was worth it because no one ever messed with him again.

NEW WORDS

embodiment
emˈbädēmənt, im-

misgiving
misˈgiviNG

kinetic
kəˈnetik

hovel
ˈhəvəl, ˈhävəl

hamper
ˈhampər

Definitions: Try matching the words in the list with the appropriate definitions. If you are stuck, check the glossary in the back of the book or the passage at the top of the page.

1.	embodiment	__________	a.	of, resulting from, or pertaining to motion
2.	misgiving	__________	b.	someone or something that perfectly represents a certain quality, idea, or feeling
3.	kinetic	__________	c.	to slow the movement, progress, or action of someone or something
4.	hovel	__________	d.	a feeling of doubt or anxiety about the consequences or outcome of something
5.	hamper	__________	e.	a small, squalid, and unpleasant dwelling

Sentences: Try to use the words above in a sentence below. Remember that a word ending may be changed or its figure of speech slightly altered.

6. Despite his original agreement to go through with the plan, Daniel had some ____________________ about his friends' idea to skip school.
7. Paul has an extremely ____________________ personality: he is always on the go and looking to explore new places.
8. Quinn's dream of becoming a famous novelist was ____________________ by his frequent bouts of laziness.
9. With the long hours that Angelica put into volunteering at the soup kitchen, she seemed to be a living ____________________ of selflessness.
10. It was surprising to see that Sean, such a refined and dapper man, lived in a(n) ____________________.

NEW WORDS

flout
flout

unremitting
ˌənriˈmitiNG

indeterminate
ˌindiˈtərmənit

exultation
ˌeksəlˈtāSHən, ˌegzəl-

sacrilege
ˈsakrəlij

Lesson 179

RICK'S REPENTANCE

Rick prayed quietly in front of a statue of Jesus Christ as the **unremitting** gaze of the holy figure stared down at him. Rick remembered with deep regret the days when he would shamelessly **flout** the religious practices that his family devotedly followed. The embarrassment and humiliation that Rick caused his family eventually got to him, and he decided to repent for his past **sacrilege**. Although the future effects of his atonement were **indeterminate** at the moment, the **exultation** Rick felt when he finally accepted Jesus as his savior was freeing.

Definitions: Try matching the words in the list with the appropriate definitions. If you are stuck, check the glossary in the back of the book or the passage at the top of the page.

1.	flout	______	a.	not exactly known, defined, or established
2.	unremitting	______	b.	a feeling of triumphant happiness
3.	indeterminate	______	c.	to openly disregard (a rule, law or convention)
4.	exultation	______	d.	a violation or misuse of what is regarded as holy or sacred
5.	sacrilege	______	e.	never stopping or lessening

Sentences: Try to use the words above in a sentence below. Remember that a word ending may be changed or its figure of speech slightly altered.

6. The vintage guitar collector considered the act of destroying one's guitar after a performance to be ______________.
7. The ______________ that Donna felt after finishing the race was euphoric.
8. Although Tim didn't do so well on the final exam, the professor still rewarded him with an A in the course for his ______________ effort throughout the semester.
9. The secret society had a(n) ______________ amount of members; nobody knew how big it truly was.
10. Nobody liked hanging out with Jack, who regularly ______________ basic manners.

Lesson 180

GUITAR SHOP

Kirk and Russell made custom guitars for a living and loved even the most menial parts of the guitar-building process, such as **interleaving** the sheets of wood for each guitar top. They completed each task with **alacrity** and care. The two friends also had a certain **synergy** when working together that allowed them to work very efficiently. However, despite their dedication and skill, Kirk and Russell were having trouble **consigning** their guitars to the local guitar store, which only sold guitars from well-known brands. Their inability to find a store to sell their guitars **stunted** their business's growth, so they decided to open their own shop instead.

NEW WORDS

consign
kən'sīn

stunted
stəntid

interleave
ˌintər'lēv

alacrity
ə'lakritē

synergy
'sinərjē

Definitions: Try matching the words in the list with the appropriate definitions. If you are stuck, check the glossary in the back of the book or the passage at the top of the page.

1. consign __________ a. an eagerness or cheerful readiness
2. stunted __________ b. to insert pages between other pages; to put something in between the layers of
3. interleave __________ c. someone or something whose development or progress is hindered
4. alacrity __________ d. to deliver something in a person's custody; to send (something) to a person to be sold; to assign permanently
5. synergy __________ e. increased effectiveness resulting from combined action

Sentences: Try to use the words above in a sentence below. Remember that a word ending may be changed or its figure of speech slightly altered.

6. Brett and Owen had an amazing ____________________ when they played music together.
7. The plant's growth was ____________________ by the insecticides used on it.
8. Winnie ____________________ four of her best paintings to the local art gallery.
9. Ronald ____________________ the pages of his storybooks with colorful illustrations.
10. Vincent read his acceptance from his dream university with ____________________.

Word Search

Lessons 171 - 180

```
Q D N V K B M D M Q N L S N P P J M J N
U E Y L N P J L D Q I U M X K W B X M M
E B Y Q R N T W T M O X L Y R V R C Y N
R A N L X Q L J P L N Y J X X K A V R W
U C T J N N B O A D I S M A N T L E J B
L L Z D Q M S M R Q A L Y G A B D K Y J
O E L N D T O N J L D H T S M Z G J B J
U N E Y E N N M A M T V T K R N E D N P
S X T R A R X C I A Z R R E I X N Z B L
K J A J Y T R Y P S O Y C T U N Y Y K X
B R L G P I N I B P G L T L Z D E P W K
Z L U N T N T A H P U I T E L J N T T N
J Z T Y G N A E R S M A V M U M N R I M
N M S L A I V I E E T D L I G Q J Y V C
M H O V E R S T R I N T E B N P S N B V
R R P L Z J L N O O N I N L D G Q U W M
Y J Y T W G U N O L H R T L I Q J T R Z
T V Q R Q M Q Z N C D P J I K E Z P L B
Z T D T W L Z N R Q W T U L V T V J X K
X P G P Q R Y Z J D Y T J E T R T Z B M
```

1 covered or concealed
2 to take something apart
3 deviating from what is normal or expected
4 traveling from place to place
5 offhand or abrupt in speech or manner
6 a person who deceives others by pretending to be someone else
7 to remain in one place in the air
8 a terrible disaster
9 a complete failure
10 one who lives a solitary existence and who often avoids people
11 complaining in an annoyed way
12 (n.) a thing assumed to be true as the basis for reasoning; (v.) to assume the truth or basis of something for the basis of reasoning or belief
13 a strong feeling of dislike
14 intense happiness and excitement
15 a feeling of doubt or anxiety about the consequences or outcome of something
16 of, resulting from, or pertaining to motion
17 never stopping or lessening
18 a feeling of triumphant happiness
19 to deliver something in a person's custody; to send (something) to a person to be sold; to assign permanently
20 an eagerness or cheerful readiness

Vocabulary Review
Lessons 171-180

Directions: Match each word with its best approximate definition. Note that definitions are not necessarily repeated verbatim from the lesson exercises.

1.	flourish	________	a.	inclined to quarrel or fight; combative
2.	oracle	________	b.	to openly disregard
3.	clemency	________	c.	a person or place noted for carrying a divine prophecy
4.	pugnacious	________	d.	existing for a long or infinite time; constantly recurring
5.	aroma	________	e.	to grow or develop in a healthy, vigorous manner
6.	intermittent	________	f.	a small, filthy, unpleasant dwelling
7.	motif	________	g.	to insert pages between blank pages in a book; to insert layers between other layers of something
8.	voluptuous	________	h.	looking or sounding sad and dismal
9.	autocrat	________	i.	a person who embodies in the flesh a sprit, idea, or abstract quality of something
10.	debris	________	j.	characterized by luxury and evoking sensual pleasure
11.	lugubrious	________	k.	the interaction of two or more entities producing a greater effect when combined than when acting alone
12.	incarnation	________	l.	occurring at irregular intervals
13.	durable	________	m.	a decorative design or pattern
14.	perennial	________	n.	violating or misusing something regarded as sacred
15.	hovel	________	o.	a ruler with absolute power
16.	hamper	________	p.	a distinctive, typically pleasant smell
17.	flout	________	q.	to hinder or impede the progress of something
18.	sacrilege	________	r.	able to withstand wear, pressure, or damage
19.	interleave	________	s.	mercy; lenience
20.	synergy	________	t.	scattered fragments of something wrecked or destroyed

A Crowd of "ISMs": A-L

When reading literature, history, art history, social sciences, politics, or philosophy, you are likely to encounter academic words ending in "ism." Here we wish to briefly define some of these meanings. This list is hardly exhaustive, but is intended to give you a sense of some common words you may see appearing in materials that you read.

abolitionism: a belief system that favors of getting rid of institutions, especially that of (formerly) slavery or capital punishment

capitalism: an economic system in which a country's trade and industry are controlled through free market exchange of wealth

communism: a model of society in which all property is publically owned and in which each person works according to his/her abilities or needs

conservatism: a belief system that supports sustaining traditional attitudes and values; in American government, it is often tied to the Republican party, which favors small government, lower taxation, and religious and family values

fascism: a nationalistic, right-wing, authoritarian system of government most widely associated with Benito Mussolini (1883-1945) in Italy.

federalism: a system of government in which powers are divided between a central (usually national) authority and smaller divisional powers

feudalism: the social system that was in place in medieval Europe, in which a lord held lands from the Crown in exchange for protection, and in which peasants and serfs lived on a lord's land and worked for him in exchange for military protection

globalism: a mode of thought or policy that envisions the whole world as a sphere of political or social influence

imperialism: a policy whereby nations expand their power into other parts of the world, often through the use of force and/or diplomacy

liberalism: a belief system associated with free political institutions and/or religious toleration together with supporting a large governmental influence in regulating capitalism and social welfare matters

libertarianism: a political philosophy that advocates only minimal public intervention in the lives of citizens

Lesson 181

NEW WORDS

sensationalism
senˈsāSHənlˌizəm

rancor
ˈraNGkər

virtuoso
ˌvərCHo͞oˈōsō

precarious
priˈke(ə)rēəs

inherent
inˈhi(ə)rənt, -ˈher-

AN UNLUCKY TALENT

Cilius Mobik is a **virtuoso** with an **inherent** talent in playing the piano. However, he is greatly underrated, and his agency is trying to do everything to put him in the spotlight where he deserves to be. The agency has started to spend big money on promoting his records and to write articles about him in several magazines. To their dismay, it has been all to no avail. The agency then decided to use **sensationalism** as a marketing tactic, making bombastic music videos of Cilius and arranging interviews where he can show off his techniques in the hope of making him famous. However, Cilius has only extracted **rancor** from the public as evidence of his natural talent remains **precarious**.

Definitions: Try matching the words in the list with the appropriate definitions. If you are stuck, check the glossary in the back of the book or the passage at the top of the page.

1.	sensationalism	__________	a.	innate; native; inbred
2.	rancor	__________	b.	unstable, unsure; uncertain; dubious
3.	virtuoso	__________	c.	the use of shocking details to cause excitement
4.	precarious	__________	d.	anger or dislike for someone
5.	inherent	__________	e.	one who excels in something especially art, or music

Sentences: Try to use the words above in a sentence below. Remember that a word ending may be changed or its figure of speech slightly altered.

6. She answered her accusers politely without a trace of ________________.
7. It is debatable whether Victor can be considered a(n) _______________ as he possesses great skills but lacks soul in his playing.
8. He could mimic printed text with alarming accuracy and dissociate the shapes and lines from their _________________ meanings.
9. The cheap tabloids relied on ________________________to increase their circulation.
10. For years, the legalization of same-sex marriage in America was on ___________________ footing, but the Supreme Court ruled in favor of it in 2015.

Lesson 182

CARLA'S UNEMPLOYMENT FIASCO

Though Carla lost her job for a **legitimate** reason – she was constantly late to work – her lack of punctuality set off a bad chain of events. First, she had to contend with her boss' **reproach** for her unprofessional behavior. Then, she had to seek **remuneration** from the government so that she could have an unemployment paycheck until she found a new job. Meanwhile, she had to adopt a **frugal** lifestyle because she was earning less than before, which alienated her from her immediate family members who expected her to continue supporting them financially. Much to their **consternation**, they could not figure out why Carla spent hours looking for her dream job rather than one that would put food on the table. Lucky for Carla, she soon found an exciting job at the local bank and stabilized her occupational and family relations.

NEW WORDS

reproach
riˈprōCH

legitimate
liˈjitəmit

consternation
ˌkänstərˈnāSHən

frugal
ˈfro͞ogəl

remuneration
riˌmyo͞onəˈrāSHən

Definitions: Try matching the words in the list with the appropriate definitions. If you are stuck, check the glossary in the back of the book or the passage at the top of the page.

1.	reproach	__________	a.	compensation; pay for a service
2.	legitimate	__________	b.	rebuke; disapproval; discredit
3.	consternation	__________	c.	sparing economically
4.	frugal	__________	d.	legal; valid; sanctioned
5.	remuneration	__________	e.	a strong feeling of surprise or sudden disappointment that causes confusion

Sentences: Try to use the words above in a sentence below. Remember that a word ending may be changed or its figure of speech slightly altered.

6. After decades of service for the army, all he gets now is a small ____________________ that is just enough for him to make ends meet.
7. When you're young, it is often wise to be ____________________ and save money rather than to spend it on lavish things.
8. They completely disregarded her request, even though it was an invariably ____________________ one.
9. Much to my ____________________, she kneeled down and proposed to me after only one awkward date.
10. Mandeville felt that he was above ____________________ and thus felt no compunction about stealing fifty dollars from his father's wallet.

Lesson 183

NEW WORDS

felicity
fə'lisətē

beneficiaries
ˌbenə'fiSHēˌerē

meddle
'medl

fraudulent
'frôjələnt

fortitude
'fôrtəˌtōōd

A GREEDY BROTHER

After Piper's father died, her brother wanted to take all the heritage and make it his own property. The family lawyer, not doing what he should have done, **meddled** in the matter and helped the brother make a **fraudulent** will deriving all money from Piper. Piper knew what the lawyer and her despicable brother were doing; she investigated the case on her own and later sent all the evidence and proof of fraud of her brother to the district prosecutor. Her **fortitude** paid off when the judge ruled that Piper was indeed one of the legitimate **beneficiaries** of her father's fortune. Piper felt **felicity** at the time the judge's decision was announced, for justice had been served. Yet she felt sorry for her brother as he was sentenced to five years in prison.

Definitions: Try matching the words in the list with the appropriate definitions. If you are stuck, check the glossary in the back of the book or the passage at the top of the page.

1.	felicity	__________	a.	cheating; dishonest
2.	beneficiaries	__________	b.	1. great happiness; 2. a talent for speaking or writing
3.	meddle	__________	c.	mental strength in facing adversity
4.	fraudulent	__________	d.	people that benefit from something, usually a trust or will
5.	fortitude	__________	e.	to be involved in activities of other people, especially when they do not want your involvement

Sentences: Try to use the words above in a sentence below. Remember that a word ending may be changed or its figure of speech slightly altered.

6. The store on the corner is being investigated by federal investigators after reports of ____________________ business activities.
7. America likes to ____________________ in other nations' business, sending troops to other countries and participating in all kinds of international disputes.
8. Tony's sudden death made all of his ____________________ millionaires.
9. Despite his belief of marriage being the end of romance, Dang is experiencing an unprecedented kind of ____________________ after marrying this woman.
10. Never once did her ____________________ waver during that long illness.

Lesson 184

THE ROVING AND UNFOCUSED STUDENT

Alison was a smart girl who was **exuberant** about going on lots of adventures. This enthusiasm was organic and resulted in many excursions; however, it prevented her from stopping to ponder the **thesis** of her history research paper. Two weeks after her professor had read this paper, he called Alison into his office and spoke to her in an **avuncular** tone. "Alison, you're a smart student, but this paper is not clear. I am going to have to give you a poor grade." Alison's eyes filled with tears as he continued. "If you persist with a life of **liberation** from your studies by traveling frequently, your grades will remain low. Going on lots of trips is not a **panacea** for all of your worries in life. Only hard word will get you academic success." Alison took the advice, quit wandering, and researched hard for her papers henceforth.

NEW WORDS

avuncular
əˈvəNGkyələr

thesis
ˈTHēsis

liberation
ˌlibəˈrāSHən

exuberant
igˈzo͞obərənt

panacea
ˌpanəˈsēə

Definitions: Try matching the words in the list with the appropriate definitions. If you are stuck, check the glossary in the back of the book or the passage at the top of the page.

1.	avuncular	________	a.	the act of freeing someone from slavery, imprisonment or oppression; a release
2.	thesis	________	b.	filled with energy and enthusiasm
3.	liberation	________	c.	like an uncle
4.	exuberant	________	d.	a remedy for all disease; a solution to all problems
5.	panacea	________	e.	a statement that someone wants to discuss or prove

Sentences: Try to use the words above in a sentence below. Remember that a word ending may be changed or its figure of speech slightly altered.

6. Love is the ________________ for all sorrows.
7. Many African-Americans look at the 1960s as a key moment in their ________________: finally, after decades of subservience, they were granted the same privileges as Caucasians in the United States.
8. Assuming thoroughly his ________________ role, Nadim takes his nephew to the movies each week.
9. My ________________ will discredit classical economics, proving its self-adjusting nature to be false.
10. The ________________ crowd rushed to greet the returning national champions in collegiate basketball.

Lesson 185

NEW WORDS

unkempt
ˌənˈkem(p)t

bankrupt
ˈbaNGkˌrəpt, -rəpt

missive
ˈmisiv

aplomb
əˈpläm, əˈpləm

plight
plīt

BERNIE'S PREDICAMENT

Once upon a time there was an **unkempt** merchant from New Hampshire named Bernie. Every day, Bernie donned a rumpled shirt and trotted into his office. One day, Bernie went into the safe near his office to look for his important papers, and discovered that all of the money he hid there was gone. "I'm practically **bankrupt**," he murmured to himself in angst. Not sure how to handle his situation, Bernie sent **missives** to his family, friends, and local authorities to articulate his **plight**. Few people were willing to assist Bernie in any way. Yet despite these setbacks, Bernie pressed on with **aplomb**. He took up three extra jobs, saved extensively for two years, and concluded that one day he might be able to have a comfortable retirement.

Definitions: Try matching the words in the list with the appropriate definitions. If you are stuck, check the glossary in the back of the book or the passage at the top of the page.

1.	unkempt	__________	a.	a written message; letter
2.	bankrupt	__________	b.	a dangerous, unfortunate, or difficult situation
3.	missive	__________	c.	confidence and skill shown especially in a difficult situation
4.	aplomb	__________	d.	having an untidy or disheveled appearance
5.	plight	__________	e.	(adj.) 1. describing a person or organization unable to pay debts; 2. depleted or impoverished; 3. completely lacking in a particular quality or value; (n.) a person deemed to be insolvent by the court system (v.) to reduce a person or organization to insolvency

Sentences: Try to use the words above in a sentence below. Remember that a word ending may be changed or its figure of speech slightly altered.

6. To blog from behind bars, Gioeli begins by writing a(n) ____________________ by hand.
7. Many people claimed that the senator was ____________________ because he wore rumpled clothes and his uncombed hair danced in the wind.
8. Lehman Brothers declared ____________________ due to their risky involvement in the derivatives market and subprime mortgage crisis.
9. She had seen the ____________________ of hundreds of people and was no stranger to death.
10. It is his ____________________ that salvages the firm in a time of such crisis.

Lesson 186

A HISTORY PARK

Alexander is trying to **tout** the investors into building a park with **archaic**-looking buildings. The park is aimed to serve people who have a **bent** for old things and history, bringing them back to the high and late medieval period when Gothic architecture was **prosperous.** Alexander suggests that the buildings need not be fully authentic, because that would involve a great deal of complex designing; they can be **derivative** from real existing Gothic buildings.

NEW WORDS

derivative
diˈrivətiv

bent
bent

archaic
ärˈkāik

prosperous
ˈprēˈpres

tout
tout

Definitions: Try matching the words in the list with the appropriate definitions. If you are stuck, check the glossary in the back of the book or the passage at the top of the page.

1.	derivative	________	a.	flourishing; successful; thriving
2.	bent	________	b.	antiquated; ancient
3.	archaic	________	c.	to persuade; to promote; to talk up
4.	prosperous	________	d.	a strong inclination; talent
5.	tout	________	e.	made up of parts from something else

Sentences: Try to use the words above in a sentence below. Remember that a word ending may be changed or its figure of speech slightly altered.

6. She can't help but feel nostalgic and perplexed standing in this marvelous castle, beholding its ________________ furniture.
7. After a(n) ________________ year, Apple stock share prices shot up by 30%.
8. The headquarters facility was ________________ as the best in the country.
9. Paul, a man of religious ________________, traveled around the world to spread the messages of Christ.
10. They say that the book lacks originality and seems to be too ________________ from other similar works.

Lesson 187

NEW WORDS

parameters
pəˈramitərz

purify
ˈpyo͝orəˌfī

mediate
ˈmēdēˌāt

savanna
səˈvanə

formulaic
ˌfôrmyəˈlāik

THE FRAMEWORK ISSUE

GreenCo and Aquapump are negotiating a deal where both firms will **purify** water from nearby water streams so that tribes in the **savanna** can utilize it for both agricultural production and everyday use. GreenCo wants to use their **formulaic** standard in controlling the quality of water which is similar to ones that GreenCo uses in other projects it has in other parts of the world. However, Aquapump refuses and insists on using original **parameters** as the standard. Without this issue, the deal would go on smoothly. Thus, to push the contract process, the firms will hire an intermediary to **mediate** this issue.

Definitions: Try matching the words in the list with the appropriate definitions. If you are stuck, check the glossary in the back of the book or the passage at the top of the page.

1.	parameters	__________	a.	to make unadulterated or clear; to free from guilt or dirt
2.	purify	__________	b.	to intervene between people in a dispute in order to bring about a resolution or agreement
3.	mediate	__________	c.	a grassy plain with few trees usually found in tropical or subtropical areas
4.	savanna	__________	d.	produced in accordance with a followed rule or style
5.	formulaic	__________	e.	guidelines that control what something is or how something should be done

Sentences: Try to use the words above in a sentence below. Remember that a word ending may be changed or its figure of speech slightly altered.

6. It is strict policy that the water here is ____________________ before it is drunk.
7. My aunt had to ____________________ the heated dispute between my parents.
8. Temperature, pressure, and density are used as ____________________ for determining the conditions of the atmosphere.
9. Unlike with math problems, there is no ____________________ way to solve interpersonal problems.
10. Sitting in his jeep looking out at the ____________________, John saw the lion fatally strike the feeble zebra.

Lesson 188

THE TAXATION MATTER

In Arizona, Republicans are trying to pass an act that would raise income tax on the middle class without raising corporate tax, which shows the politicians' **propensity** to favor the rich. Although this act is **feasible** as no problem will occur in the implementation of it, it is **deleterious** to the state's economy as most people will have less money to consume and further invest; it also will widen the income gap between the rich and the poor. Many opposing lobbyists, as well as politicians, are trying to stop this act from passing. If it is passed, it will be very arduous to **repeal**, and other **contiguous** states may make the same mistake.

NEW WORDS

propensity
prəˈpensətē

contiguous
kənˈtigyo͞oəs

feasible
ˈfēzəbəl

deleterious
ˌdeliˈti(ə)rēəs

repeal
riˈpēl

Definitions: Try matching the words in the list with the appropriate definitions. If you are stuck, check the glossary in the back of the book or the passage at the top of the page.

1.	propensity	__________	a.	to revoke or annul (a vote or congressional act)
2.	contiguous	__________	b.	capable of being done, effected
3.	feasible	__________	c.	damaging or harmful
4.	deleterious	__________	d.	touching; adjacent
5.	repeal	__________	e.	a strong natural tendency to do something

Sentences: Try to use the words above in a sentence below. Remember that a word ending may be changed or its figure of speech slightly altered.

6. Your plan sounds ideal, but whether it is ______________________ is another story.
7. The imposition of tariffs can be ______________________to one's economy as it creates both production and consumption distortion.
8. The United States is ______________________ with Canada and Mexico, but not with Italy and Mongolia.
9. The homophobic Westboro Baptist Church wants the legalization of same-sex marriage ______________________.
10. Marginal ______________________ to consume shows how much a population is willing to spend given a level of income.

NEW WORDS

somnolent
ˈsämnələnt

coward
ˈkou-ərd

unerring
ˌənˈəriNG, -ˈer-

conspire
kənˈspīr

meager
ˈmēgər

Lesson 189

ACCOMPLICE BETRAYAL

Chuck was a very poor guy, trying to get by every day on his **meager** paycheck. One day, he thought of robbing a bank so that he could get rich. He then held a talk with some of his close poor friends, asking if any of them wanted to be his partner in crime. He **conspired** with them to come up with a plan. Sadly, the meeting was **somnolent** because he thought his plan was **unerring** and didn't listen to anyone's opinions. All of the friends left, except one. On the day of the robbery, the plan went wrong, and they were arrested. While being interrogated, his friend **cowardly** said that Chuck was the master of the plan so as to get less time in jail. Chuck really regretted what he had done, but it was too late.

Definitions: Try matching the words in the list with the appropriate definitions. If you are stuck, check the glossary in the back of the book or the passage at the top of the page.

1.	somnolent	__________	a.	deficient in quantity or quality
2.	coward	__________	b.	to secretly plan to something harmful or illegal
3.	unerring	__________	c.	likely to induce sleep
4.	conspire	__________	d.	a person who shows a shameful lack of courage
5.	meager	__________	e.	always right or accurate

Sentences: Try to use the words above in a sentence below. Remember that a word ending may be changed or its figure of speech slightly altered.

6. Thriftymart pays its part-time employees a(n) ____________________ $7.25 an hour.
7. The television series *Game of Thrones* is so twisted and full of people who ____________________ to replace their king with someone easily influenceble.
8. Cheating on his girlfriend and abandoning her when she is pregnant proves that Khoa is just another despicable ____________________.
9. The sermon was so ____________________ that even the most eager listeners quickly dozed off after it was underway.
10. With ____________________ conviction, Samuel knew that pursuing a second doctorate was a good career move for him.

Lesson 190

AN UNEXPECTED SUCCESS

Britney had always been known as a little **obtuse** and lazy. She did not study well, and people thought she would amount to nothing in life. But Britney dreamed of being a fashion store owner, and her **intuition** told her that she could pursue this dream. Despite opposition from her family and friends, Britney decided to use her savings to open a clothing store selling **ersatz** brand name clothing. For her dream, Britney became a determined and **diligent** young lady, working very hard to run her store and never losing faith despite the first few months of sporadic sales. Later on, her hard work did pay off, and people were **nonplussed** to see that her store was the most popular store for young working women in town.

NEW WORDS

intuition
ˌint(y)o͞oˈiSHən

obtuse
əbˈt(y)o͞os, äb-

diligent
ˈdiləjənt

nonplussed
nänˈpləst

ersatz
ˈerˌsäts, -ˌzäts, erˈzäts

Definitions: Try matching the words in the list with the appropriate definitions. If you are stuck, check the glossary in the back of the book or the passage at the top of the page.

1.	intuition	________	a.	painstaking; assiduous
2.	obtuse	________	b.	utterly perplexed
3.	diligent	________	c.	being a usually artificial and inferior substitute
4.	nonplussed	________	d.	stupid or unintelligent
5.	ersatz	________	e.	quick and ready insight; the ability to know something without having proof

Sentences: Try to use the words above in a sentence below. Remember that a word ending may be changed or its figure of speech slightly altered.

6. Despite meticulous instruction from the lecturer, Hieu is simply too ____________________ to comprehend the model.
7. "How on earth did you know he was going to ask you out?"
   "Just my ____________________."
8. Chinese companies are gifted at manufacturing ____________________ goods and selling them at cheap prices.
9. Justin was utterly ____________________ when he learned that his work had become the fourteenth most read paper in the field.
10. Daddy teaches me to be ____________________, persevering through all the storms that life might bring.

Crossword Puzzle

Lessons 181-190

ACROSS

1 confidence and skill shown especially in a difficult situation
8 a strong inclination; talent
9 compensation; pay for a service
11 to persuade; to promote; to talk up
12 one who excels in something especially art, or music
13 to intervene between people in a dispute in order to bring about a resolution or agreement
16 cheating; dishonest
17 capable of being done, effected
18 touching; adjacent
19 stupid or unintelligent
20 a written message; letter

DOWN

2 guidelines that control what something is or how something should be done
3 a strong feeling of surprise or sudden disappointment that causes confusion
4 always right or accurate
5 unstable, unsure; uncertain; dubious
6 the act of freeing someone from slavery, imprisonment or oppression; a release
7 quick and ready insight; the ability to know something without having proof
10 mental strength in facing adversity
14 to secretly plan to something harmful or illegal
15 a statement that someone wants to discuss or prove

Vocabulary Review
Lessons 181-190

Directions: Match each word with its best approximate definition. Note that definitions are not necessarily repeated verbatim from the lesson exercises.

1.	rancor	________	a.	anger or dislike for someone
2.	inherent	________	b.	innate; native; inbred
3.	legitimate	________	c.	thrifty; economical
4.	frugal	________	d.	causing harm or damage
5.	felicity	________	e.	very old or old-fashioned; no longer in use but used to convey an old-fashioned flavor
6.	meddle	________	f.	materialistically or intellectually successful; doing well financially
7.	avuncular	________	g.	like an uncle
8.	panacea	________	h.	showing care and consciousness in one's responsibilities
9.	unkempt	________	i.	to interfere in something that is generally not one's concern
10.	plight	________	j.	lacking in quality or quantity
11.	archaic	________	k.	to remove contaminants from something
12.	prosperous	________	l.	an inclination or natural tendency to behave in a particular way
13.	purify	________	m.	a dangerous, hard, or very unfortunate situation
14.	savanna	________	n.	so surprised and confused that one does not know how to react
15.	propensity	________	o.	conforming to the law or rules; able to be defended with justification
16.	deleterious	________	p.	a person who lacks the courage to endure unpleasant things
17.	coward	________	q.	a grassy plain typically found in tropical and subtropical climate zones
18.	meager	________	r.	having an untidy or disheveled appearance
19.	diligent	________	s.	extreme happiness
20.	nonplussed	________	t.	a solution or remedy for all illnesses or problems

A Crowd of "ISMs": M-Z

Here we continue our list of important "ism" words often found in intellectual literature.

modernism:	**a style or movement in the arts or architecture that breaks with classical forms**
nationalism:	**patriotic feelings in support of a particular country, often as superior over other countries**
nihilism:	**rejecting all religious and moral principles, often associated with the belief that life has no meaning**
postmodernism:	**an intellectual style and concept in arts and intellectual scholarship that represents a departure from modernism, often revealing a general distrust of grand theories and ideologies**
realism:	**the belief in representing people, situations, or things in such a way that appears true to life**
socialism:	**a theory in economics and politics emphasizing that the production, distribution, and exchange of goods should be regulated by the whole community; a transitional state between capitalism and communism**

structuralism:	**a belief that in human cognition, behavior, and culture, there is an underlying pattern or structure that organizes and reflects patterns and contrasts underneath a superficial diversity**
surrealism:	**a movement in early twentieth century art and literature aimed at juxtaposing things irrationally in order to stimulate creative thought**
totalitarianism:	**a system of government that is heavily centralized and with a dictator which requires total subservience to the state**

NEW WORDS

induce
in'd(y)o͞os

extract
ik'strakt

thwart
THwôrt

lingering
'liNGg(ə)riNG

ogle
'ōgəl

Lesson 191

AN OBSTINATE WITCH

Manny was not very good at getting dates with girls in college. Every day, he would sit in the cafeteria and **ogle** the most attractive ladies he saw. Then he would come up to their table and ask them out on a romantic date. Regularly they **thwarted** his attempts to secure a date, and told him that he was **inducing** a sense of nausea in them. Still, Manny retained a **lingering** hope that one day he would actually get a date with one of these pretty girls. Finally, on his last dinner at college, Manny was able to **extract** the phone number of Lauren, a girl he'd been thinking about for years, in a conversation. Quickly realizing that she had accidentally given Manny her phone number, Lauren ran to the store after dinner and immediately changed her number. Manny, as usual, was left hopeless.

Definitions: Try matching the words in the list with the appropriate definitions. If you are stuck, check the glossary in the back of the book or the passage at the top of the page.

1.	induce	________	a.	to frustrate or baffle; to oppose
2.	extract	________	b.	staying beyond expected time
3.	thwart	________	c.	to stare at in a manner showing sexual desire
4.	lingering	________	d.	1. to remove or take out; 2. to obtain a substance or resource by a special method
5.	ogle	________	e.	to cause someone to do something

Sentences: Try to use the words above in a sentence below. Remember that a word ending may be changed or its figure of speech slightly altered.

6. Many radical groups in the world use torture to ________________ information from people they suspect of crimes.
7. Even though Shonté was dumped by her boyfriend, there remained a(n) ________________ hope in her mind that he would one day return for her.
8. Harvey ________________ the young girl because he liked her but was too socially insecure to ask her out.
9. If you want people to do things for you, you have to ________________ them by giving incentives.
10. The Republicans consistently try to ________________ any plan that Democrats posit by giving falsified facts to the public.

Lesson 192

A REGRETTABLE DISOBLIGATION

After a God-defying **impertinence,** the city of Oglipayas was cursed into a **moribund** state where all resources and water suddenly ran out. Herculias, the hero of the city, tried to save the day by finding the long lost holy diamond ring and offering it to their god in a **consecrated** ceremony. Their god read the Oglipayans' **cognitive** thoughts and judged that they all earnestly sought forgiveness, so their god rescinded his curse, making the city return to its normal state. The Oglipayans were so **jubilant** that they held parties for 300 consecutive days. They never disobeyed their god again.

NEW WORDS

cognitive
ˈkägnətiv

impertinence
imˈpərtnəns

consecrated
ˈkänsiˌkrāt

moribund
ˈmôrəˌbənd, ˈmär-

jubilant
ˈjo͞obələnt

Definitions: Try matching the words in the list with the appropriate definitions. If you are stuck, check the glossary in the back of the book or the passage at the top of the page.

1.	cognitive	________	a.	dedicated to a sacred purpose
2.	impertinence	________	b.	rejoicing; triumphant; joyous
3.	consecrated	________	c.	irrelevance, inappropriateness, or absurdity
4.	moribund	________	d.	involving conscious mental activities
5.	jubilant	________	e.	no longer active or effective; very sick; close to death

Sentences: Try to use the words above in a sentence below. Remember that a word ending may be changed or its figure of speech slightly altered.

6. Fred was ____________________ when he heard that his team had won the state soccer match.
7. Everybody could feel the ____________________ mood radiating from the duchess when her baby was declared a prince.
8. A solid course in buyer behavior will walk students through all the ____________________ stages that a customer goes through before he or she purchases a good.
9. Writing with this kind of ____________________ won't get you anywhere in the real world.
10. People have seen Courtney going to various auditions recently; she must be trying to revive her ____________________ career.

Lesson 193

NEW WORDS

avarice
ˈavəris

inertia
iˈnərSHə

engrossing
enˈgrōsiNG

arduous
ˈärjo͞oəs

pedagogy
ˈpedəˌgäjē, -ˌgägē

A VENERABLE PROFESSION

Pedagogy is a profession that is **engrossing** for many who like academics. It is so captivating because teachers have to be altruistic and passionate about their job. Teachers generally lack **avarice** as well – even though they work long and **arduous** hours, they do not expect to be paid big money. Teachers sometimes feel tired and frustrated too, but they never show any **inertia**. They always try to be energetic and dedicated to their students.

Definitions: Try matching the words in the list with the appropriate definitions. If you are stuck, check the glossary in the back of the book or the passage at the top of the page.

1.	avarice	__________	a.	very difficult; challenging
2.	inertia	__________	b.	greed
3.	engrossing	__________	c.	the art, science, or profession of teaching
4.	arduous	__________	d.	1. a tendency to do nothing or remain unchanged; resistance to change in some physical property; 2. (in physics) a property where an object remains in its existing rest state or in straight line motion unless acted upon by an external force
5.	pedagogy	__________	e.	absorbing all of one's attention and interest

Sentences: Try to use the words above in a sentence below. Remember that a word ending may be changed or its figure of speech slightly altered.

6. Governmental ____________________ in structural reforms has cost Vietnam further potential GDP growth.
7. To get where he is now, Justin had to go through a great deal of turmoil and tons of ____________________ work.
8. His knowledge of ____________________ was displayed when he spoke at length about the various theories about teaching small classes of students.
9. The new book was so ____________________ that I sat for six hours straight and read it in its entirety.
10. Many CEOs are plagued by ____________________ and a thirst for power.

Lesson 194

A PRESIDENTIAL UPSET

Everyone thought that the president would win reelection because he was an **incumbent** who had done an excellent job leading during his first term. He also had **recourse** to a lot of wealthy donors who wished to **perpetuate** his image as the appropriate leader to continue fighting for their rights. But his rival, an upstart from Boston, had a **vibrant** message of how to strengthen the economy and democracy in the country by helping the lower and middle classes. His speeches **astounded** voters and, in the end, the incumbent lost the election. The support of the masses allowed for a sea change in politics.

NEW WORDS

astound
əˈstound

recourse
ˈrēˌkôrs, riˈkôrs

vibrant
ˈvībrənt

incumbent
inˈkəmbənt

perpetuate
pərˈpeCHo͞oˌāt

Definitions: Try matching the words in the list with the appropriate definitions. If you are stuck, check the glossary in the back of the book or the passage at the top of the page.

1.	astound	__________	a.	showing great life, activity, and energy; very bright and strong
2.	recourse	__________	b.	someone currently holding office
3.	vibrant	__________	c.	to astonish; to flabbergast; to amaze
4.	incumbent	__________	d.	1. to make something continue indefinitely; 2. to preserve something valued from oblivion or extinction
5.	perpetuate	__________	e.	an opportunity or choice to use or do something in order to deal with a problem or situation

Sentences: Try to use the words above in a sentence below. Remember that a word ending may be changed or its figure of speech slightly altered.

6. Often it is easier for a(n) ______________________ to win reelection because he or she is currently in office and has experience with his or her position.
7. The professor ______________________ teaching his impractical method at the cost of the department's reputation.
8. What ______________________ me the most is how a department in such a prestigious university can treat its students so unprofessionally and unfairly.
9. The dispute was settled without ______________________to law.
10. Freddie Mercury is widely regarded as the best live performer of his era for being consistently ______________________ at his events.

Lesson 195

NEW WORDS

pundit
ˈpəndit

unflappable
ˌənˈflapəbəl

amenable
əˈmēnəbəl, əˈmen-

miscreant
ˈmiskrēənt

belabor
biˈlābər

AN OUTSPOKEN, DISCONTENTED CITIZEN

Isaac is an expert in current affairs, and he is not **amenable** to the way the government has handled many recent issues. With the support of multitude of people in academia and the political world, Isaac has begun giving speeches that **belabor** how incompetent the government is. The **pundits** who defend the government, however, depict him as a **miscreant**. With great aplomb, Isaac seems to be **unflappable** in his steadfast commitment to his beliefs; he carries on with his series of speeches, demanding that the government do its job right.

Definitions: Try matching the words in the list with the appropriate definitions. If you are stuck, check the glossary in the back of the book or the passage at the top of the page.

1.	pundit	__________	a.	to repeat an idea or argument to emphasize it
2.	unflappable	__________	b.	a person who behaves badly or in a way that breaks the law
3.	amenable	__________	c.	an expert who usually gives speeches in public
4.	miscreant	__________	d.	open and responsive to suggestion
5.	belabor	__________	e.	imperturbable; to be able to remain calm in a difficult situations

Sentences: Try to use the words above in a sentence below. Remember that a word ending may be changed or its figure of speech slightly altered.

6. While some professors are ____________________ to giving take-home final exams, others insist on taking a three-hour test in class.
7. Some ____________________ could always be found to comment, and imagination supplied what newspapers feared to print.
8. He just likes to show that he can do magic and then ____________________ the point through talking excessively about his skill.
9. People could not believe that Jane dated a(n) ____________________ like James.
10. He prided himself on being ____________________ in even the most chaotic situation.

Lesson 196

FREE-MINDED ARCHAEOLOGIST

Erica was a **neophyte** archaeologist who recently has been on her first dig to unearth part of an **extinct** civilization located near the Euphrates River. Together with a team, Erica **traversed** over forty square kilometers hoping to excavate something important. Nothing was found, however, and the team leader intimated that his colleagues had become **indolent**. But Erica thought she had seen an artifact along the way. Her team leader did not want to hear her queries, and insisted on her **subordination** to his commands. But Erica broke with the team and began to dig. Amazingly, she unearthed a talisman from a long departed civilization!

NEW WORDS

subordination
səˌbôrdnˈāSHən

neophyte
ˈnēəˌfīt

indolent
ˈindələnt

extinct
ikˈstiNG(k)t

traverse
trəˈvərs

Definitions: Try matching the words in the list with the appropriate definitions. If you are stuck, check the glossary in the back of the book or the passage at the top of the page.

1.	subordination	__________	a.	lazy
2.	neophyte	__________	b.	to cross; to cut across
3.	indolent	__________	c.	no longer existing
4.	extinct	__________	d.	a beginner, greenhorn, tyro
5.	traverse	__________	e.	the act of placing in a lower rank or position

Sentences: Try to use the words above in a sentence below. Remember that a word ending may be changed or its figure of speech slightly altered.

6. Unlike Samuel, who had been a seasoned member of congress, Barry was a(n) ____________________ only beginning his first term.
7. Many of the factory workers here are ____________________: they snooze on the job rather than produce the widgets that we had hoped they would create.
8. That homosexuality will make the human race ____________________ is an unqualified argument.
9. The refusal to allow women to be educated was part of society's long history of ____________________of women to men.
10. The candidates ____________________ the state throughout the campaign.

Lesson 197

NEW WORDS

emblem
ˈembləm

trepidation
ˌtrepiˈdāSHən

Byzantine
ˈbizənˌtēn, bəˈzan-, -ˌtīn

disrepute
ˌdisrəˈpyo͞ot

vagary
ˈvāgərē

THE CHANGE OF IMAGE

Nina fell into **disrepute** after her company was found to be guilty of ethical misconduct. The firm decided to change its old image by changing its **emblem**. The process of designing a new emblem had to be deliberately and carefully planned; it could not be just a **vagary** that popped out of someone's mind. After extensive rumination, Nina finally contrived a new emblem to represent her company. This new emblem was **Byzantine**, having a lot of complicated patterns and tiny details. It is completely different stylistically from the old logo. Nina hopes that the new sign will help revive her business, but she has some **trepidation** about whether a new tag can truly resurrect her company.

Definitions: Try matching the words in the list with the appropriate definitions. If you are stuck, check the glossary in the back of the book or the passage at the top of the page.

1.	emblem	__________	a.	lack of good reputation
2.	trepidation	__________	b.	whim; unusual idea
3.	Byzantine	__________	c.	a person or thing that represents an idea
4.	disrepute	__________	d.	labyrinthine; intricate
5.	vagary	__________	e.	feeling of fear that something may happen

Sentences: Try to use the words above in a sentence below. Remember that a word ending may be changed or its figure of speech slightly altered.

6. With much ____________________, the circus clown jumped through a ring of fire.
7. The President fell into ____________________ after multiple allegations of extramarital affairs.
8. Captain America is the ____________________ of the United States of America: disciplined, responsible, and perseverant.
9. It really is Mother Nature's ____________________ if the temperature drops to zero degrees one summer night.
10. Day after day, tape after tape, I became more enthralled with the ____________________ plot of his life.

Lesson 198

THE MOTIVATION REGENERATION

After the death of the beloved former CEO, the firm's employees fell into a **morbid** state. They worked with lethargy and discouragement. The Board of Directors could not let this situation **habituate** for they knew if it did it would make the firm **founder**. Thus, they started to look for a new CEO who not only was excellent in strategic management but also could bring a renewed **vitality** to the firm. The Board was **elated** to find a new CEO who satisfied what they were looking for in only two weeks. The employment of the new CEO gave the employees a revived motivation and a sense of direction.

NEW WORDS

founder
ˈfoundər

vitality
vīˈtalitē

morbid
ˈmôrbəd

habituate
həˈbiCHo͞oˌāt

elate
iˈlāt

Definitions: Try matching the words in the list with the appropriate definitions. If you are stuck, check the glossary in the back of the book or the passage at the top of the page.

1.	founder	________	a.	cheerless; unpleasant; morose
2.	vitality	________	b.	(n.) someone who establishes an institution or settlement; (v.) 1. to collapse or fail (of a plan or endeavor); 2. to fill with water and sink (of a ship)
3.	morbid	________	c.	to make or become accustomed or used to something
4.	habituate	________	d.	to make (someone) extremely happy
5.	elate	________	e.	vigorousness; exuberance

Sentences: Try to use the words above in a sentence below. Remember that a word ending may be changed or its figure of speech slightly altered.

6. "This is such a marvelous and joyous wedding! Look at how ____________________ the couple is!"
7. The chief difficulty experienced by the administration was to ____________________ the Arabs and Nubas, both naturally warlike, to a state of peace.
8. After the death of the lead guitarist, it was clear to see that the band had lost its ____________________.
9. I have a(n) ____________________ fear of spiders.
10. Opening a new campus on the other side of town doesn't make sense with the fact that their training programs are ____________________.

Lesson 199

NEW WORDS

astonishing
ə'stäniSHiNG

sparing
'spe(ə)riNG

fragrant
'frāgrənt

perseverance
ˌpərsə'vi(ə)rəns

mimic
'mimik

A SUPERFICIAL GUY

Chuck is a poor guy, but he always tries so hard to do shallow things. He **mimics** celebrities' behaviors and spends almost everything he has on perfumes so that he can be **fragrant** all the time. In spending on other things in life, however, he is very **sparing**, calculating every possible way to save some money. It is **astonishing** to see how he uses his **perseverance** to earn very little money then squanders it on unnecessary things. People wish that he would one day wake up and become pragmatic.

Definitions: Try matching the words in the list with the appropriate definitions. If you are stuck, check the glossary in the back of the book or the passage at the top of the page.

1.	astonishing	________	a.	aromatic; perfumed; scented
2.	sparing	________	b.	to imitate; to copy
3.	fragrant	________	c.	economical; frugal; meager
4.	perseverance	________	d.	determination; endurance
5.	mimic	________	e.	startling; stunning; amazing

Sentences: Try to use the words above in a sentence below. Remember that a word ending may be changed or its figure of speech slightly altered.

6. The mortgage officer showed reluctance to make a loan to the ________________ couple who are trying to save up enough for a house.
7. Even if you are smart, lacking ________________ and grit will not bring you success.
8. Despite coming across as child-like at first, Peter has shown to have ________________ compassion and consideration for others.
9. She has a talent for ________________ famous actresses; she now makes a living out of impersonation.
10. The soup was ________________ with herbs and spices.

Lesson 200

SAILING RECOLLECTION

After an **exhaustive** day sailing through stormy waters, our ship finally was **becalmed** as the winds off the Florida coast subsided. The ship's captain, too, **severed** his relationship with two lazy crewmen who did not appropriately manage the boat facilities. With this newfound tranquility, the passengers on our sailboat finally began to delight in their time at sea. Sleeping on a boat was never something that I suspected that I would like, but my initial **leery** feelings about this endeavor dissipated amidst this spell of tranquility. Gleefully I "commiserated" with my sailing buddies as I soaked up the sun. How I wished I could stay on this boat forever relaxing while a **proxy** did my work back at home.

NEW WORDS

exhaustive
igˈzôstiv

sever
ˈsevər

becalm
biˈkä(l)m

leery
ˈli(ə)rē

proxy
ˈpräksē

Definitions: Try matching the words in the list with the appropriate definitions. If you are stuck, check the glossary in the back of the book or the passage at the top of the page.

1.	exhaustive	________	a.	suspicious; wary
2.	sever	________	b.	to deprive (a ship) of wind necessary to move it
3.	becalm	________	c.	the authority to represent someone else, especially in voting
4.	leery	________	d.	complete; comprehensive; full-scale
5.	proxy	________	e.	1. to divide by cutting or slicing; 2. to terminate or break off a connection or relationship

Sentences: Try to use the words above in a sentence below. Remember that a word ending may be changed or its figure of speech slightly altered.

6. Quan was ____________________ of her neighbors for they were acting dubiously.
7. ____________________ at sea, the ship sat motionless for hours.
8. When representing your clients in court, you have to use an appropriate ____________________ or else your case will not be coherent.
9. After a(n) ____________________ search of our house, we still had not found the cat.
10. After breaking up with Annie, John blocked her phone number and disengaged with all of their mutual friends, thus ____________________ all connections with her.

Word Search

Lessons 191-200

S E V I T S U A H X E P B L
U T R E P I D A T I O N Q B
B G N I S S O R G N E L V Y
O C O N S E C R A T E D E N
R V I T D I I M E T N L G F
D I Z N M N E N A D B T R N
I T S I C L U U D A N A T B
N A M U B U T B P O G U E T
A L Y M O E M P I R L L O E
T I E X P U A B A R A E C F
I T M R O L D N E B O U N E
O Y E R F R T R O N D M L T
N P T N J J P R A N T G M V
M B U N W N J P I L O M T M

1 to cause someone to do something
2 to stare at in a manner showing sexual desire
3 dedicated to a sacred purpose
4 no longer active or effective; very sick; close to death
5 absorbing all of one's attention and interest
6 very difficult; challenging
7 someone currently holding office
8 1. to make something continue indefinitely; 2. to preserve something valued from oblivion or extinction
9 imperturbable; to be able to remain calm in a difficult situations
10 to repeat an idea or argument to emphasize it
11 the act of placing in a lower rank or position
12 lazy
13 a person or thing that represents an idea
14 feeling of fear that something may happen
15 (n.) someone who establishes an institution or settlement; (v.) 1. to collapse or fail (of a plan or endeavor); 2. to fill with water and sink (of a ship)
16 vigorousness; exuberance
17 aromatic; perfumed; scented
18 to imitate; to copy
19 complete; comprehensive; full-scale
20 the authority to represent someone else, especially in voting

Vocabulary Review
Lessons 191-200

Directions: Match each word with its best approximate definition. Note that definitions are not necessarily repeated verbatim from the lesson exercises.

1.	thwart	________	a.	full of energy or enthusiasm; colorful
2.	lingering	________	b.	a beginner, novice, greenhorn, tyro
3.	cognitive	________	c.	to shock or surprise immensely
4.	jubilant	________	d.	an unexpected change in a situation or in someone's behavior
5.	avarice	________	e.	steadfastness in something despite difficulty or delay in achieving success
6.	pedagogy	________	f.	lasting for a long time, staying or hanging around
7.	astound	________	g.	no longer in use or existence
8.	vibrant	________	h.	an expert in a field who frequently has his or her opinions solicited
9.	pundit	________	i.	to become ecstatically happy
10.	miscreant	________	j.	greed
11.	neophyte	________	k.	the method of practice of teaching
12.	extinct	________	l.	cautious due to realistic suspicions
13.	disrepute	________	m.	to frustrate or baffle; to oppose
14.	vagary	________	n.	characterized by an interest in unpleasant things such as death and disease
15.	morbid	________	o.	held in low esteem by the public
16.	elate	________	p.	feeling or expressing great happiness; triumphant
17.	astonishing	________	q.	to divide by cutting off
18.	perseverance	________	r.	a person who is ill-behaved or who breaks the law
19.	sever	________	s.	extremely surprising or amazing; impressive
20.	leery	________	t.	concerning the process of acquiring, assessing, and assimilating knowledge

Long Live Latin!

Though Latin is, for all intents and purposes, a dead language outside of Vatican City, many of its phrases still show up in modern English texts (though less frequently on standardized tests). Below is a list of some common Latin phrases that are used in English together with their meanings.

a posteriori:	**reasoning from effects to causes**
a priori:	**reasoning from causes to effects**
ad hoc:	**for this purpose (for a specific purpose)**
ad hominem:	**a specific attack on an individual's values based on emotion rather than on reason**
ad nauseum:	**to a sickening extent**
bona fide:	**in good faith; sincerely**
carpe diem:	**seize the day**
ceteris paribus:	**all things being equal**
et cetera (etc.):	**and the rest; and so forth**
ex libris:	**from the library (of...)**
habeas corpus:	**writing saying someone has been brought legally before a court to decide whether detaining such an individual is legal**
ibid.:	**in the same place in a book (short for Latin ibidem)**
in loco parentis:	**in the place of a parent**
in situ:	**in position; in its original place**
in vitro:	**in a test tube (literally: in glass)**
in vivo:	**within a living organism**
inter alia:	**amongst other things**
mea culpa:	**through my own fault**
non sequitur:	**a conclusion or inference that doesn't follow from its premises (literally: it does not follow)**
per annum:	**by the year**
per capita:	**by the heads; for each person taken individually**
per diem:	**by the day; per day; for each day**
per se:	**by or in itself**
post mortem:	**an autopsy (literally: after death)**
prima facie:	**at first sight; on the face of it**

quid pro quo: one thing for another; something for something
semper fidelis: always faithful
sine qua non: indispensible
vice versa: the positions being reversed; if the positions were reversed

Idiomatic Expressions I

Idiomatic expressions are phrases whose meaning does not convey the literal sense of the words in the expression. For example, telling someone to "break a leg" does not convey that you wish someone to have a personal injury. Rather, the phrase "break a leg" means "good luck," and is typically said to someone before a theatrical or musical performance. English has hundreds of idioms, and many native speakers only know a fraction of them. Below and in two additional Idiomatic Expressions sections is a list of some common English idiomatic expressions. These lists are by no means exhaustive, but should help you get a sense of some commonly said idioms.

Idiomatic Expression	Meaning/Example
to break a leg	Said to wish someone good luck in a musical or theatrical performance. My mother told me to break a leg before I played the lead role in my school play.
to go postal	Going completely insane, often involving violence A man went postal last week and punched three grocery store clerks in the face for no apparent reason
to break the ice	To initiate social interaction or conversation After three minutes of sitting in silence in the theater group, Laura broke the ice and asked how everyone's day was.
once in a blue moon	Rarely, not very often. Suzanna is into fitness and eats ice cream only once in a blue moon.

to get up on the wrong side of the bed	**To feel irritable; to be in a bad mood; to have a bad day from the moment it begins** **Marylou must have gotten up on the wrong side of the bed; normally she is very friendly, but she seems to be screaming at everyone today.**
crocodile tears	**Showing emotion insincerely.** **The politician showed crocodile tears at his electoral opponent's funeral. He wasn't truly sad to see his opponent die; on the contrary, he was thrilled to have less competition!**
piece of cake	**Finding a task to be extremely easy.** **Today's calculus test was a piece of cake; I know I got 100% and the test only took fifteen minutes to complete!**
(every cloud has a) silver lining	**No matter how bleak a situation is, there is always some positive element in it.** **Even though Nitu lost her corporate job and was unemployed for three months, she saw the silver lining around her circumstances, discovered a newfound love for comedy, and is now a successful comedian.**
to pass the buck	**To not assume responsibility for something and designate that responsibility to someone else.** **Rather than assuming responsibility for explaining corporate losses, the CEO passed the buck to his CFO to explain the downturn.**
to throw a curve(ball)	**To confuse someone by doing something tricky or unexpected.** **Sean threw his brothers a curve when his date for prom was not the girl that they expected but rather his best male friend.**

to hit the sack/hit the hay	**To fall asleep** **After a long day of walking around the amusement park, the kids hit the hay as soon as they arrived at home.**
to bring down the house	**To evoke heavy applause and cheers** **Jessica's singing brought down the house last night; everyone was captivated by her amazing voice.**
to leave no stone unturned	**To search every possible place for something.** **Shri left no stone unturned in the hotel when she looked for her keys that had gone missing.**
back to the drawing board	**Time to start from the beginning again** **When all of Kel's plans to get a date with Liz failed, he went back to the drawing board to ponder new ideas to get her on a date.**
to spill the beans	**To reveal a secret or surprise** **Jason spilled the beans when he told his sister that everyone was throwing her a surprise birthday party at 6PM at her favorite restaurant.**
out to lunch	**Not alert, uninformed, giddy** **I think Linda was out to lunch at the business conference on Friday; she did not follow a single rule that employees were commanded to follow at the meeting.**
to feather one's nest	**To acquire wealth for oneself, usually by exploiting others to obtain said wealth.** **The CEO feathered his nest by taking key employees out to lunch and flattering them in order to win their approval.**

to let sleeping dogs lie	**To not instigate trouble; to not incite something that could cause trouble.** **Martha encouraged her brother to let sleeping dogs lie and not provoke the school bully, who already had been expelled from school for beating her up.**
to take with a grain of salt	**To not take seriously** **Everyone takes Mrs. Angotti's criticisms with a grain of salt, for she exaggerates everything she says.**
to pull one's (own) weight	**To do one's fair share of the work** **In a healthy team project each team member must pull his or her (own) weight.**
to show one's hand	**To reveal one's true intentions** **Nobody believed that Alice really loved James; she showed her hand when she admitted to her friends that James was only a good boyfriend because he had money to buy her all of the expensive clothes that she wanted.**
left holding the bag	**Left to take all the blame for something** **Paula and James jointly robbed a bank. But when the police arrived, Paula quickly escaped out the back door and left James holding the bag as the sole culprit in the robbery.**
ivory tower	**A place that feels sealed off from the real world** **Many people argue that professors live in an ivory tower because their research often centers strictly on theoretical issues rather than pragmatic ones.**

to cut corners	**To take shortcuts or find easier or cheaper ways of doing things** **A bad business will try and cut corners on its budget by using staff and resources of subpar quality and charging full price for its services.**

Lesson 201

STRICT HISTORY TEACHER

My history teacher, Mr. Knee, is a **stickler** for details. He is very concerned about ensuring that students remember dates of all major historical events and will **harangue** students who forget to do their homework or who cannot remember famous quotes **verbatim**. He is also not **moderate** in his class rules, for students who arrive late without an excuse note will automatically receive a detention. Trying to cut corners in Mr. Knee's class is a challenge for the **guileless**: one needs to truly be an expert at deception to get away with anything in this class.

NEW WORDS

stickler
ˈstik(ə)lər

verbatim
vərˈbātəm

guileless
ˈgīllis

moderate
ˈmäd(ə)rət (adj.; n.); ˈmäd(ə)rət (v.)

harangue
həˈraNG

Definitions: Try matching the words in the list with the appropriate definitions. If you are stuck, check the glossary in the back of the book or the passage at the top of the page.

1.	stickler	________	a.	(adj. and adv.) in exactly the same words as used originally
2.	verbatim	________	b.	a person who demands a certain quality or type of behavior
3.	guileless	________	c.	to lecture at length in an aggressive, critical manner
4.	moderate	________	d.	(adj.) 1. average in amount, intensity, or degree; 2. not politically radical; (n.) a person who does not hold radical views; (v.) 1. to make less extreme, intense or violent; 2. to preside over
5.	harangue	________	e.	innocent and without deception

Sentences: Try to use the words above in a sentence below. Remember that a word ending may be changed or its figure of speech slightly altered.

6. Leon was a(n) ____________________ for details: he needed to hear precise details about all of his business plans.
7. Kiet's father ____________________ him to do his homework since he was lazy.
8. Most animals prefer ____________________ weather to extreme heat or cold.
9. Court stenographers are supposed to copy peoples' statements in court ____________________, thus creating an exact transcript of what transpired.
10. The ____________________ entrepreneur was easily duped by his competitors.

NEW WORDS

verbalize
ˈvərbəˌlīz

bliss
blis

queer
kwi(ə)r

dilate
ˈdīˌlāt, dīˈlāt

arable
ˈarəbəl

Lesson 202

DROUGHT CONCERNS

It is a little **queer** that Juan, who usually has difficulty **verbalizing** his feelings, was so fiery and articulate in articulating his thoughts on the recent drought. He told us all that months without rain had made local **arable** land unsuitable for farming, and that citizens in the agricultural valley may be toiling away for at least three years after the drought ends before they could have any **blissful** experience in reaping a giant harvest. His anger over the lack of hydration seems to have **dilated** his blood vessels, for Juan was flush red when he stated his views.

Definitions: Try matching the words in the list with the appropriate definitions. If you are stuck, check the glossary in the back of the book or the passage at the top of the page.

1.	verbalize	__________	a.	suitable for growing crops
2.	bliss	__________	b.	to make wider or larger; to open
3.	queer	__________	c.	to express ideas or feelings in words, often by speaking out loud
4.	dilate	__________	d.	strange; odd
5.	arable	__________	e.	perfect happiness; great joy

Sentences: Try to use the words above in a sentence below. Remember that a word ending may be changed or its figure of speech slightly altered.

6. Because they receive so little rainfall, most desert lands are not ____________________.
7. When I go to the eye doctor, he puts drops in my eye to ____________________ my pupil and examine my widened eyes better.
8. I always feel ____________________ when I am eating my favorite chocolate cake and vanilla ice cream.
9. It can be difficult to date someone who has difficulty ____________________ his or her feelings: it is important to express how we feel so that others understand us.
10. It is definitely ____________________ to wear a bathing suit to a state funeral.

Lesson 203

RESTAURANT RELOCATION

I fear that my favorite restaurant's seemingly **impromptu** decision to move from an urban location to a rural hideaway may be a **retrograde** step for the establishment. Currently the restaurant is flourishing downtown, where many people admire its savory dishes. A sudden move away from the city is **consonant** neither with the restaurant's metropolitan ambience nor with its clientele's cosmopolitan mindset. And it seems like the restaurant may have to **exhort** its customers to travel far if it wants to sustain business. Many people find the restaurant's decision to move to be **blasphemous** for a business whose stated mission is to make city life more relaxing.

NEW WORDS

consonance
ˈkänsənəns

exhort
igˈzôrt

retrograde
ˈretrəˌgrād

blasphemous
ˈblasfəməs

impromptu
imˈpräm(p)ˌt(y)o͞o

Definitions: Try matching the words in the list with the appropriate definitions. If you are stuck, check the glossary in the back of the book or the passage at the top of the page.

1. consonance ________ a. to urge or encourage one to do something
2. exhort ________ b. (adj. and adv.) done without being planned, organized, or rehearsed
3. retrograde ________ c. agreement or compatibility between opinions or actions
4. blasphemous ________ d. directed or moving backwards; reversed
5. impromptu ________ e. sacrilegious; against God or sacred things

Sentences: Try to use the words above in a sentence below. Remember that a word ending may be changed or its figure of speech slightly altered.

6. It is ____________________ to pick your nose and eat your boogers before the Queen of England.
7. To an observer on Earth, most planets occasionally exhibit ____________________ motion: occasionally they travel backward on their path.
8. Rather than preparing his speech, Jason spoke in ____________________ form.
9. Mark ____________________ his sister to run for mayor because so many people felt that she was the right person for the job.
10. Dylan is an excellent businessman because his behaviors are always ____________________ with his vows: he always follows through on his word.

NEW WORDS

proponent
prə'pōnənt

dismissive
dis'misiv

mystified
'mistə,fīd

glutton
'glətn

distressed
dis'trest

Lesson 204

WOMEN'S RIGHTS ACTIVIST

I am **mystified** about how Cassandra, a **proponent** of women's rights, could be so **dismissive** of her feminist peers. Because my curiosity urged me to explore the issue, I decided to probe Cassandra on her views. Cassandra intimated that she was **distressed** by many of her feminist peers because they valued advancing women's rights at the cost of curtailing men's rights. For Cassandra, who was a **glutton** for equality on all issues, the best type of female advocate is one who recognizes that men and women are equals: bringing down the status of one sex to boost the other was, to her, downright terrible.

Definitions: Try matching the words in the list with the appropriate definitions. If you are stuck, check the glossary in the back of the book or the passage at the top of the page.

1.	proponent	__________	a.	(for someone) to be utterly bewildered or perplexed
2.	dismissive	__________	b.	a person who is usually fond of or eager for something (often food)
3.	mystified	__________	c.	a person who advocates a project, cause, or theory
4.	glutton	__________	d.	suffering from anxiety, sorrow, or pain
5.	distressed	__________	e.	feeling that something is unworthy of consideration

Sentences: Try to use the words above in a sentence below. Remember that a word ending may be changed or its figure of speech slightly altered.

6. My neighbor was ____________________ by how roses grew on my lawn in the middle of January.
7. Huey is a(n) ____________________ for chocolate; he cannot resist cocoa.
8. A good teacher is never ____________________ of his/her students' intellectual needs, for teachers should always look to ensure that a student is challenged.
9. Amber was ____________________ when she heard the sad news that her boyfriend had been injured in a train accident.
10. As a major ____________________ of the movement to abolish fast food restaurants in Italy, Gianna pushed to have all chain restaurants in Milan closed.

Lesson 205

TEMPLE VISIT FAILURE

Because the threat of an avalanche was **imminent**, we were unable to take the **serpentine** road up to the mountain temple. This was particularly disappointing, for the temple contains a **replica** of a famous fourth century statue of a local deity. My brother, despite **fulsome** remarks to our tour guide, was unable to reschedule the temple visit to the next week, which made him depressed. The circumstances are truly unfortunate because our travel agency, which is renown for its **unimpeachable** commitment to satisfying tourist wishes, was unable to make a temple trip materialize during our journey.

NEW WORDS

serpentine
ˈsərpənˌtēn, -ˌtīn

imminent
ˈimənənt

unimpeachable
ˌənimˈpēCHəbəl

fulsome
ˈfo͞olsəm

replica
ˈreplikə

Definitions: Try matching the words in the list with the appropriate definitions. If you are stuck, check the glossary in the back of the book or the passage at the top of the page.

1.	serpentine	__________	a.	unable to be doubted or questioned; entirely trustworthy
2.	imminent	__________	b.	flattering to an excessive degree
3.	unimpeachable	__________	c.	winding or twisting
4.	fulsome	__________	d.	an exact model or copy of something
5.	replica	__________	e.	about to happen

Sentences: Try to use the words above in a sentence below. Remember that a word ending may be changed or its figure of speech slightly altered.

6. The road up the mountain is ____________________ and turns endlessly.
7. The brilliant François built a breathtaking ____________________ of the Eiffel Tower out of toothpicks.
8. Most Americans revere president Abraham Lincoln (1809-1865) for his candor and ____________________ behavior.
9. Judging from the sky's rapidly darkening color, a storm is likely ____________________.
10. While giving compliments can be nice, excessively ____________________ behavior is usually not a good quality.

Lesson 206

NEW WORDS

immaterial
ˌi(m)məˈti(ə)rēəl

insulate
ˈins(y)əˌlāt

unsolicited
ˌənsəˈlisitid

lodging
ˈläjiNG

gilded
ˈgildid

GOLDEN PALACE

Because all of the objects in the king's palace are **gilded**, **lodging** in the palatial estate is restricted to people only of noble birth. Furthermore, because of the exorbitant price of these objects, the palace is **insulated** by scores of guards who, every hour, prevent thieving commoners from showing up **unsolicited**. It is **immaterial** whether one's intentions are genuine or conniving, as nobody who is not regal is welcome beyond the palace gates.

Definitions: Try matching the words in the list with the appropriate definitions. If you are stuck, check the glossary in the back of the book or the passage at the top of the page.

1.	immaterial	__________	a.	to use a material to protect something from the elements or heat loss
2.	insulate	__________	b.	unimportant under the circumstances; irrelevant
3.	unsolicited	__________	c.	covered thinly with gold leaf or gold paint
4.	lodging	__________	d.	not requested; done voluntarily
5.	gilded	__________	e.	a place where someone lives or stays temporarily

Sentences: Try to use the words above in a sentence below. Remember that a word ending may be changed or its figure of speech slightly altered.

6. When taking a long road trip it is helpful to find ____________________ for each night to sleep in.
7. Many homes in cold climates have material in their attics to ____________________ them from the cold.
8. Many people find Claudia offensive because she always offers ____________________ advice to people on how to live their lives.
9. Many objects in the Sultan of Brunei's palace are ____________________; because of their high value, common people are not allowed to touch them.
10. Whether you are rich or poor is ____________________ to whether you will be faithful in a relationship.

Lesson 207

THEATRICAL DEBUT

After memorizing all of her lines and reading through the **minutiae** of the play script, Janine was finally ready to go on stage. She was to play a major role in *Frankenstein*, a piece that embodied the spirit of **romanticism** at its height. As she awaited the stagehand's **cue** to go on a stage, she could feel a sense of excitement **pervading** the auditorium. In five minutes she would be on stage reciting her lines, waiting for the **stimulus** of the orchestra to get her dancing after her initial soliloquy was complete.

NEW WORDS

minutiae
məˈn(y)o͞oSHēˌē, -SHēˌī

pervade
pərˈvād

cue
kyo͞o

romanticism
rōˈmantəˌsizəm, rə-

stimulus
ˈstimyələs

Definitions: Try matching the words in the list with the appropriate definitions. If you are stuck, check the glossary in the back of the book or the passage at the top of the page.

1.	minutiae	__________	a.	a thing said or done that serves as a signal for action
2.	pervade	__________	b.	the state or quality of expressing feelings, inspiration, and subjectivity over reason
3.	cue	__________	c.	to spread through and be perceived in all parts of a place
4.	romanticism	__________	d.	small, precise, or trivial details of something
5.	stimulus	__________	e.	1. a signal or event that evokes a reaction by a tissue or organ; 2. a thing that rouses activity in someone or something; 3. an exciting or interesting quality

Sentences: Try to use the words above in a sentence below. Remember that a word ending may be changed or its figure of speech slightly altered.

6. A skunk's odor often ____________________ through entire neighborhoods.
7. Neil is so lazy; he only works if provided with a major ____________________.
8. Most CEOs of giant corporations do not like to have countless hours of their time wasted pouring over ____________________ of their business.
9. Books that emphasize feeling and passion over reason are said to deal with hallmark ideas of the ____________________ movement.
10. Alice is to go on stage and sing as soon as Harry gives her the ____________________ to perform.

NEW WORDS

crux
krəks, kro͝oks

piecemeal
ˈpēsˌmēl

relegate
ˈreləˌgāt

innuendo
ˌinyo͞oˈendō

prevalent
ˈprevələnt

Lesson 208

ACADEMIC INTEGRITY

Cheating has become a **prevalent** problem at many of America's top universities. Academic officials have noted the increased sense of academic misconduct, and think that a growing apathy for scholarly values lay at the **crux** of the problem. Students, they believe, have **relegated** pursuing knowledge to a lower priority than developing a professional identity. Many of academicians' **innuendos** reveal a great disgust at this trend. Sadly, efforts to restore academic integrity on campuses have been **piecemeal** and have resulted in no large-scale revival of scholarly values. We can only hope that students will once again begin to cherish their studies.

Definitions: Try matching the words in the list with the appropriate definitions. If you are stuck, check the glossary in the back of the book or the passage at the top of the page.

1.	crux	__________	a.	to consign to an inferior mark or position
2.	piecemeal	__________	b.	widespread in a particular area at a particular time
3.	relegate	__________	c.	a suggestive, allusive, often disparaging remark
4.	innuendo	__________	d.	characterized by unsystematic partial measures taken over a period of time
5.	prevalent	__________	e.	the decisive or most important point at issue

Sentences: Try to use the words above in a sentence below. Remember that a word ending may be changed or its figure of speech slightly altered.

6. In many Southeast Asian countries, motorbikes are ____________________: they constitute well over half of the vehicles on the roads.
7. Ho Chi Minh City has grown through ____________________ development projects over the last two decades.
8. Though Shad's argument was replete with details, the ____________________ of his point was that California taxes must be lowered.
9. It was hard for Monica to ignore Theodore's ____________________ to come to his room for a little private chat.
10. Many intellectual snobs often ____________________ lowbrow humor to pure puerile crap.

Lesson 209

CHEMICAL POLLUTANT BILL

Next week congress is set to **ratify** a bill that will implement a new **taxonomy** for classifying poisonous liquid chemicals. The reason for this change is that many environmentalists think that the current scheme to identify chemicals is not clear enough to provide **prognoses** for many hazardous toxic situations. Because so many liquid chemicals **contaminate** our waters, we need a more explicit system for identifying the chemicals by their potency. Supporters of the new bill have expressed **unbounded** enthusiasm for it and are eager to see it implemented immediately.

NEW WORDS

contaminate
kən'tamə,nāt

prognosis
präg'nōsəs

taxonomy
tak'sänəmē

ratify
'ratə,fī

unbounded
,ən'boundid

Definitions: Try matching the words in the list with the appropriate definitions. If you are stuck, check the glossary in the back of the book or the passage at the top of the page.

1.	contaminate	__________	a.	to sign or give formal consent to a contract, treaty, or agreement to make it formally valid
2.	prognosis	__________	b.	to make impure by adding a polluting substance
3.	taxonomy	__________	c.	limitless
4.	ratify	__________	d.	forecasted outcome of a situation or disease
5.	unbounded	__________	e.	branch of science dealing with the classification of organisms; the classification of something; a scheme of classification

Sentences: Try to use the words above in a sentence below. Remember that a word ending may be changed or its figure of speech slightly altered.

6. In order for the bill to be ____________________, a majority of the senators must vote in favor of it.
7. Carl Linnaeus (1707-1778) is the father of our ____________________ system; in creating it, he assigned two Latin words to classify each living organism he knew.
8. Tanya had ____________________ enthusiasm for the equestrian show: nothing could limit her passion for horses and their riders.
9. The doctor's fortunate ____________________ was that Bruce did not have cancer as he initially expected.
10. Chemicals from the nearby factory have ____________________ drinking water to the point of it being non-potable.

NEW WORDS

reprieve
riˈprēv

interminable
inˈtərmənəbəl

uncouth
ˌənˈko͞oTH

varied
ˈve(ə)rēd

inhabit
inˈhabit

Lesson 210

PROBOSCIS MONKEYS

After what seemed like an **interminable** two years of working on her dissertation, Ivona was thrilled to get a month-long break. It was something of a necessary **reprieve** for her, as she was finally able to **inhabit** a space other than her university library. So she decided to go to Hawaii for that month. Her vacation reminded her that, aside from research, she had such **varied** interests as scuba diving, theater, rock climbing, and fine dining. But after having been sheltered away from people for so long, some fellow tourists that she met on her vacation found her to be a bit **uncouth**. Such experiences reminded Ivona that, even though she is inundated with academic work, it is important to maintain a social life.

Definitions: Try matching the words in the list with the appropriate definitions. If you are stuck, check the glossary in the back of the book or the passage at the top of the page.

1.	reprieve	________	a.	to live in or occupy a place or environment
2.	interminable	________	b.	lacking good manners, refinement, or grace
3.	uncouth	________	c.	showing a number of different types of elements
4.	varied	________	d.	unending; unceasing
5.	inhabit	________	e.	(n.) a cancellation or postponement of punishment; (v.) to cancel or postpone the punishment of someone

Sentences: Try to use the words above in a sentence below. Remember that a word ending may be changed or its figure of speech slightly altered.

6. After thirty weeks of work, six days a week, Shalina was happy to receive a(n) ____________________ so she could relax.
7. Three different Native American tribes once ____________________ this region of upstate New York.
8. Florin has such ____________________ interests as scuba diving, cooking, reading medieval French poetry, and stamp collecting.
9. It is ____________________ to belch in the middle of a wedding ceremony.
10. The baby's crying felt ____________________: for twenty straight minutes, the little boy on the bus whined incessantly.

Crossword Puzzle

Lessons 201-210

ACROSS

3 branch of science dealing with the classification of organisms; the classification of something; a scheme of classification
10 forecasted outcome of a situation or disease
13 a place where someone lives or stays temporarily
15 (for someone) to be utterly bewildered or perplexed
16 lacking good manners, refinement, or grace
17 directed or moving backwards; reversed
18 innocent and without deception
19 unable to be doubted or questioned; entirely trustworthy
20 not requested; done voluntarily

DOWN

1 the decisive or most important point at issue
2 a thing said or done that serves as a signal for action
4 to consign to an inferior mark or position
5 about to happen
6 (adj. and adv.) in exactly the same words as used originally
7 small, precise, or trivial details of something
8 to make wider or larger; to open
9 suffering from anxiety, sorrow, or pain
11 (adj. and adv.) done without being planned, organized, or rehearsed
12 unending; unceasing
14 to express ideas or feelings in words, often by speaking out loud

Vocabulary Review
Lessons 201-210

Directions: Match each word with its best approximate definition. Note that definitions are not necessarily repeated verbatim from the lesson exercises.

1.	stickler	________	a.	twisting; winding
2.	harangue	________	b.	to lecture someone in a lengthy and aggressive manner
3.	bliss	________	c.	an allusive or indirect remark or hint
4.	arable	________	d.	to make something impure by adding a substance
5.	exhort	________	e.	to make a piece of legislation (contract, treaty, etc.) officially valid
6.	blasphemous	________	f.	a person who advocates a theory, proposal, or project
7.	proponent	________	g.	to spread through and exist in every part of a region
8.	glutton	________	h.	a person who is excessively fond of something, especially food
9.	serpentine	________	i.	a thing said or done to serve as a signal – often in acting
10.	replica	________	j.	land suitable for growing crops
11.	insulate	________	k.	to live in or occupy a place
12.	gilded	________	l.	a person who insists on a certain quality or type of behavior
13.	pervade	________	m.	sacrilegious or profane
14.	cue	________	n.	to protect from the loss of heat or entry of sound; to protect from the unpleasant elements of something
15.	innuendo	________	o.	covered thinly with gold leaf or paint
16.	prevalent	________	p.	to strongly encourage someone to act
17.	contaminate	________	q.	widespread in a certain area at a particular time
18.	ratify	________	r.	total joy or happiness
19.	reprieve	________	s.	a short rest from an undesirable situation
20.	inhabit	________	t.	an exact copy or model of something

Idiomatic Expressions II

This list is a continuation of common idiomatic expressions. It is the second unit in a three-part sequence.

Idiomatic Expression	Meaning/Example
sour grapes	Something that one cannot have and, as a consequence, one disparages it as if it were not desirable. Even though Ann fairly lost the debate for which she had spent months preparing, others perceived her subsequent dismissal of it as being meaningless as sour grapes.
wouldn't be caught dead	To never do something because it would be too embarrassing to be caught doing it Ahuva said she wouldn't be caught dead eating food out of a garbage can.
to cost an arm and a leg	To be very expensive Hamburgers at the new restaurant cost an arm and a leg. They're at least twice as expensive as any other burger in town.
writing on the wall	Likelihood that something bad will happen I could see the writing on the wall concerning Horatio's divorce when he and his wife began fighting every day.

to go up in smoke	**To be spoiled or wasted** **Martha's secret plans to retire went up in smoke after Hailey announced them to the entire office staff.**
on the dot	**Exactly on time** **Marcus is always punctual for afternoon meetings; he always shows up for his scheduled 2PM appointment at 2:00 on the dot.**
tongue in cheek	**To say something without serious intention** **Gene said tongue in cheek that he would date Kelly, but when Kelly actually asked him out he felt somewhat uncomfortable.**
through thick and thin	**Through good times and bad times** **Fair-weather friends will leave someone in times of trouble, but a good friend will stand by your side through thick and thin.**
to keep a stiff upper lip	**To not let unfortunate things upset you; to not act upset (even if you might be)** **Even though Eileen's sister burned all of her textbooks before her final exams, Eileen kept a stiff upper lip and was civil to her sister. She also went to the library to study her notes and to use books available to the public in order to prepare for her tests.**

not playing with a full deck	**Not operate in a rationally or mentally sound manner** **When Tom told his boss that cookies were not selling because they were too expensive and his boss decided to raise the sale price of cookies in an attempt to boost sales, Tom became convinced that his boss was not playing with a full deck.**
to burn the midnight oil	**Stay up very late at night working** **Chris burned the midnight oil cramming formulas into his head for Fridays' physics exam.**
to wear one's heart on one's sleeve	**To reveal one's emotions too clearly** **Marco wore his heart on his sleeve when he told his bosses how depressed he was at work and how his coworkers were stealing pencils from his desk.**
Achilles heel	**A(n) (often deadly) weakness in spite of a great strength** **Although Greg was an eloquent speaker, his Achilles heel was public oratory: he stuttered when speaking to large groups.**
off the beaten path	**Not well known or popular with many people** **Eddie's Diner is a fabulous restaurant that is off the beaten path: since it is four miles from the highway and in the middle of the countryside, only locals and well-informed travelers are aware of its splendor.**
to lay one's cards on the table	**To reveal one's true intentions; to be candid about one's position on an issue** **Rather than trying to defend her brother's sloth, Barbara lay her cards on the table concerning her brother's indolence: "My brother is lazy and cannot finish tasks on time," she bluntly told his clientele.**

without rhyme or reason	**For no rational purpose or reason** **Yolanda is a pretty unpredictable person. Often she will lose her temper and become violent without rhyme or reason.**
at the drop of a hat	**Immediately, instantly** **The king expected his chefs to serve him a five-course meal at the drop of a hat: he expected that if he merely snapped his fingers, plates of meat and vegetables would be on their way to his throne.**
to make a long story short	**To get to the point; to avoid a longwinded explanation** **Though Elena was sick of her boyfriend dating other girls and flirting with random people, she preferred brevity when she addressed the problem to him. Rather than delineating her complaints, she said, "To make a long story short, you're not faithful. That's why our relationship is now over."**
to bring home the bacon	**To earn a salary or bring home money earned on a job** **Lukas took a big job at a consulting firm so that he could bring home the bacon and support his family.**
to carry the day	**To be successful; to win a competition** **Even though Martin pointed out a fallacy in Fred's logic, Fred's overall argument carried the day.**
on pins and needles	**Anxious or in suspense** **Scott was on pins and needles waiting for his exam results to get posted.**

to steal someone's thunder	**To take the credit and accolades for something that another person does** **Although Derek wrote a brilliant paper with penetrating insights into the causes of the Industrial Revolution, his adviser stole Derek's thunder and accepted much intellectual credit for guiding Derek's thought processes.**
to have the upper hand	**To have a position of power and control over someone else** **Even though Rajib worked hard and wanted a raise, he was tactful in requesting one from his boss, who held the upper hand in making decisions about the former's salary.**

Lesson 211

NEW WORDS

recriminations
riˌkriməˈnāSHənz

expound
ikˈspound

devour
diˈvou(ə)r

mawkish
ˈmôkiSH

aural
ˈôrəl

RESTAURANT DRAMA

People came from far and wide to **devour** the excellent food prepared by Andreas. His Dutch restaurant was thriving, and people **expounded** in great detail their perceived reasons for his success. One day, however, a client ordered a bowl of bean soup from Andreas, but she received a plate of apple strudel instead. Having very little patience, the client mocked Andreas' **aural** skills. She accused Andreas of being mean-spirited and ignorant, and he responded with **recriminations** that she was being overly hostile and insensitive. She then sat in the restaurant crying for over an hour, worrying Andreas that her **mawkish** nature was a real problem. Only when Andreas offered her a free coffee did the customer cheer up and recant for overreacting.

Definitions: Try matching the word in the box with the appropriate definition. If you are stuck, check the glossary in the back of the book or the passage at the top of the page.

1.	recriminations	__________	a.	to explain and present a theory or idea systematically and in detail
2.	expound	__________	b.	to eat or read with great intensity and in large quantity
3.	devour	__________	c.	accusations in response to those from someone else
4.	mawkish	__________	d.	of or related to the ear or sense of hearing
5.	aural	__________	e.	sentimental in a feeble or discomforting way

Sentences: Try to use the words above in a sentence below. Remember that a word ending may be changed or its figure of speech slightly altered.

6. Though Archie can read and write Japanese well, his ____________________ skills need some work; listening exercises remain a challenge for him.
7. Good lawyers are able to ____________________ upon their arguments with ease in a courtroom.
8. When the students accused their teacher of grading them unfairly, the teacher made ____________________ about her students' poor study habits to the principal.
9. We watched Jimmy ____________________ three pizzas and two ice cream sundaes for lunch; he must have been very hungry!
10. People accused Jerry of being ____________________ when she cried nearly every day for six months after her boyfriend dumped her.

Lesson 212

AN ACADEMIC CALLING

Emily's primary choice for a **vocation** was to become a university history professor. When she was in college, she **inquired** regularly about which new academic books had just appeared on the market. During her graduate school career, nothing could satiate her **craving** for reading new books and writing analyses of them. Many professors heralded her doctoral thesis on the Great Depression as a **masterful** work that profoundly impacted how scholars see economic trends in modern America. Before long, and perhaps somewhat **unwittingly**, a somewhat green Emily found herself receiving tenure track offers at many of the world's most prestigious universities because of her sustained scholarly labor.

NEW WORDS

masterful
ˈmastərfəl

unwitting
ˌənˈwitiNG

inquire
inˈkwīr

vocation
vōˈkāSHən

craving
ˈkrāviNG

Definitions: Try matching the word in the box with the appropriate definition. If you are stuck, check the glossary in the back of the book or the passage at the top of the page.

1.	masterful	__________	a.	a person not aware of the full facts; not done purposefully
2.	unwitting	__________	b.	a powerful desire for something
3.	inquire	__________	c.	a strong feeling of suitability for a career or occupation; a person's employment or job
4.	vocation	__________	d.	powerful and able to control others; performed or performing extremely skillfully
5.	craving	__________	e.	to ask information from someone

Sentences: Try to use the words above in a sentence below. Remember that a word ending may be changed or its figure of speech slightly altered.

6. Dale was a(n) ____________________ accomplice in yesterday's bank robbery. She did not know that her friend hid stolen money in the trunk of her car.
7. Choosing a(n) ____________________ can be an ordeal for someone who is extremely talented and has several possible prosperous career paths.
8. Hilda had a(n) ____________________ for a hamburger and drove to the local diner at four in the morning in order to have one.
9. If you are allergic to peanuts, it is imperative that you ____________________ whether peanut products are used to make the meals that you order at a restaurant.
10. Shayna did a(n) ____________________ job in the school debate: the other candidates simply could not challenge her or find any aporiae in her arguments.

Lesson 213

NEW WORDS

placebo
plə'sēbō

voluminous
və'lo͞omənəs

microcosm
'mīkrə͵käzəm

simulate
'simyə͵lāt

gaffe
gaf

FAYE'S SPEAKNG PROBLEM

Faye is a brilliant woman, but she has difficulty speaking in public. Though her intentions are genuine, she is prone to making **gaffes** that obstruct her ability to forge a stellar environmental science career. This is especially painful, as she has done a **voluminous** amount of research on carbon emissions and has **simulated** dozens of experiments in her lab to bolster her findings. If her department at the local university can be seen as a **microcosm** of the academic field at large, then she surely will not be advancing far on her career path because of her verbal blunders. Her friends claimed to give her pills to help her become a better speaker, but in fact these pills were merely **placebos**: they were only a thoughtful means of motivating her to have the courage to present. With a little luck, Faye will garner the courage to deliver better talks soon.

Definitions: Try matching the word in the box with the appropriate definition. If you are stuck, check the glossary in the back of the book or the passage at the top of the page.

1.	placebo	__________	a.	large in volume; occupying much space
2.	voluminous	__________	b.	a harmless pill prescribed for psychological benefit rather than for physiological effect
3.	microcosm	__________	c.	an unintentional remark or act lavishing embarrassment on its originator; a blunder
4.	simulate	__________	d.	a community, situation, or place regarded as encapsulating key qualities of something larger
5.	gaffe	__________	e.	to imitate the character or appearance of

Sentences: Try to use the words above in a sentence below. Remember that a word ending may be changed or its figure of speech slightly altered.

6. Brian believed that the pills he took helped him lose weight, but in actuality they were merely ____________________; he shed pounds from keeping a strict diet.
7. Before trekking into outer space, potential astronomers are often placed into man-made structures that ____________________ an environment devoid of gravity.
8. Many shareholders suspect that Shaolaine will not be made the company's new CEO because she is prone to making ____________________ at public events.
9. Yetta's dissertation is ____________________: it is over 600 pages long.
10. It would be unfair to call New York City a(n) ____________________ of American life because a large country's values cannot be appropriately reflected by the people and behaviors of a single city.

Lesson 214

SKILLED MARRIAGE COUNSELOR

Gerald is a **veteran** marriage counselor who, in the course of his thirty-year career, has guided many dissatisfied couples away from divorce. Usually he can sense when a couple is on the verge of falling apart by honing in on their **semantics** during therapy sessions. He can also tell when at least one member of a couple assumes a fake or hostile **persona** to incite agitation. Many of the couples he has seen reconcile their problems, and claim that he is among the shrewdest **arbitrators** of relationships that they know. If you feel that you are approaching the **advent** of divorce, you should contact Gerald for help.

NEW WORDS

veteran
ˈvetərən, ˈvetrən

advent
ˈadˌvent

persona
pərˈsōnə

semantic
səˈmantik

arbitrator
ˈärbiˌtrātər

Definitions: Try matching the word in the box with the appropriate definition. If you are stuck, check the glossary in the back of the book or the passage at the top of the page.

1.	veteran	__________	a.	the aspect of one's character presented to or perceived by others
2.	advent	__________	b.	related to meaning in logic or language
3.	persona	__________	c.	an independent person or body appointed to settle a dispute
4.	semantic	__________	d.	the arrival of a notable thing, person, or event
5.	arbitrator	__________	e.	1. a person experienced in a particular field; 2. a person who has served in the military

Sentences: Try to use the words above in a sentence below. Remember that a word ending may be changed or its figure of speech slightly altered.

6. Businessmen much prefer looking at cold, hard data to analyzing ____________________ terms that saturate academic studies of management.
7. Though this is my first time playing paintball, I have received good advice on how to play from my friend Jake, who is a(n) ____________________ at the sport.
8. Historians note that the ____________________ of computers dates back to the calculating machine that French mathematician Blaise Pascal (1623-62) made in 1642.
9. Because they were unable to negotiate peaceably, Carla and Erik required a(n) ____________________ to help dissolve their estate following their divorce.
10. Even though Jeanne was not a very friendly person, her job as a customer service representative forced her to adopt an affable ____________________ at work.

Lesson 215

NEW WORDS

deficient
diˈfiSHənt

fetter
ˈfetər

inordinate
iˈnôrdn-it

flora
ˈflôrə

natty
ˈnatē

TROUBLE IN BIOLOGY CLASS

Jacob was a good student overall, but he was often **deficient** in science skills. Because of this, he spent an **inordinate** amount of time reviewing notes and rereading his textbook for botany class. Sometimes he would even spend the majority of a weekend practically **fettered** to his desk so that he could absorb the content of his coursework. Now, with an intricate test on **flora** classification on the horizon, Jacob is more worried than ever. He knows that, even if he studies voraciously, gets a good night sleep, and wears **natty** clothes to his exam, he may still not succeed. But with a little fortitude and inspiration, he should have some success in botany.

Definitions: Try matching the word in the box with the appropriate definition. If you are stuck, check the glossary in the back of the book or the passage at the top of the page.

1.	deficient	__________	a.	smart and fashionable (usually of a person or of clothing)
2.	fetter	__________	b.	unusually or disproportionally large; excessive
3.	inordinate	__________	c.	the plants of a particular region, habitat, or geological period
4.	flora	__________	d.	to restrain with chains or manacles (literally or metaphorically)
5.	natty	__________	e.	lacking in a specified ingredient, ability, or quality

Sentences: Try to use the words above in a sentence below. Remember that a word ending may be changed or its figure of speech slightly altered.

6. Despite being brothers, the ____________________ gap between Mark and Larry's intellectual abilities is remarkable.
7. Nothing could ____________________ Tran's insatiable thirst for money.
8. It is shocking how, although Bali and Lombok are only about 35 kilometers apart, their ____________________ differs significantly.
9. Students who are not educated in quality schools are often ____________________ in their verbal and mathematics skills.
10. All of the ladies in the retirement home fawned over Jason's ____________________ appearance and charming personality.

Lesson 216

CONTENTIOUS CARTOONIST

Just this past year a new cartoonist has had a strip appear in the local newspaper. The cartoons, which feature an **anthropomorphized** cat, have caused quite a stir. Initially, elderly people became **incensed** when the cartoon cat stated derogatory things about old people. More recently, handicapped citizens have adopted a **surly** attitude toward the cartoonist after the fictitious cat mocked people with dyslexia and agoraphobia. At the rate things are going, this cartoon cat may cause a major **upheaval** at the local newspaper office. I am unclear as to why the local press has not ceased printing the cartoon, especially since its editors **profess** to be egalitarian and humane people.

NEW WORDS

upheaval
ˌəpˈhēvəl

anthropomorphize
ˌanTHrəpəˈmôrˌfīz

incensed
inˈsenst

surly
ˈsərlē

profess
prəˈfes, prō-

Definitions: Try matching the word in the box with the appropriate definition. If you are stuck, check the glossary in the back of the book or the passage at the top of the page.

1.	upheaval	___________	a.	a violent or sudden disruption to something
2.	anthropomorphize	___________	b.	to attribute human characteristics to the behavior of an animal, object, or god
3.	incensed	___________	c.	very angry; enraged
4.	surly	___________	d.	bad-tempered and unfriendly
5.	profess	___________	e.	to claim openly (and often falsely) that one possesses a certain feeling or quality

Sentences: Try to use the words above in a sentence below. Remember that a word ending may be changed or its figure of speech slightly altered.

6. Unlike Silas, who has a pleasant disposition, Louisa is often quite ______________________.
7. Kwame was ______________________ when he heard that his brother had stolen his favorite pair of shoes and sold them for extra spending money on spring break.
8. It is easy to ______________________ to be an altruistic person; it is much harder to actually be so in real life.
9. Artists almost always ______________________ cartoon characters: usually such creatures wear human clothes, stand upright, and/or speak human languages.
10. Because of the recent ______________________ in the Middle East, travelers are being urged to avoid taking leisure trips in that region.

Lesson 217

NEW WORDS

waft
wäft, waft

authenticate
ô'THenti,kāt

grotesque
grō'tesk

multifarious
,məlt(ə)'fe(ə)rēəs

incision
in'siZHən

PLASTIC SURGERY DILEMMA

Generally speaking, Kylie was a pretty girl with **multifarious** likeable traits, yet there was one physical handicap that served as a hindrance: she had a gigantic, bulbous nose. People openly mocked this **grotesque** facial feature, thus causing Kylie to feel insecure about her appearance. As a result, she decided to undergo rhinoplasty. For weeks she tried to **authenticate** the credentials of the best surgeons in town before finally going under the knife. With skill and care, the town's best surgeon made an **incision** near Kylie's nose and began work. Kylie looks very different now, and I can enjoy watching her drink hot cocoa as the steam from her piping hot drink **wafts** out of its cup across her face. Not everyone with a big nose need remain ugly forever!

Definitions: Try matching the word in the box with the appropriate definition. If you are stuck, check the glossary in the back of the book or the passage at the top of the page.

1.	waft	__________	a.	many and of various different types
2.	authenticate	__________	b.	comically or repulsively ugly; incongruous to a shocking degree
3.	grotesque	__________	c.	a surgical cut made into the skin or flesh
4.	multifarious	__________	d.	to prove or show something to be genuine
5.	incision	__________	e.	to pass or cause gently to pass through the air

Sentences: Try to use the words above in a sentence below. Remember that a word ending may be changed or its figure of speech slightly altered.

6. It is often an elaborate task to ____________________ a copy of a rare antique book.
7. The doctor made a(n) ____________________ into the patient's chest at the beginning of the surgery.
8. Most colleges are ____________________ institutions: they have many different parts and aspects to them.
9. On a clear day, I can see steam out of factory chimneys ____________________ through the air.
10. In recent decades, income disparity in the United States has become ____________________: the rich now have so much while the poor have so little.

Lesson 218

THE TOUCHING NOVELLA

When my friend was in college, he wrote an autobiographical novella about a romantic endeavor that he had. The work tells the story of a man who met a woman in a café, and, after **numerous** exchanges, asked her out on a date. But the two were opposites in their lifestyles: he led a **Spartan** existence while she bathed in opulence. Initially they got along well, but gradually the **reciprocity** between them broke down and their relationship ended. In order to savor the moment, my friend wrote a beautiful **vignette** about the experience, for if he could not have the girl he could at least have a beautiful piece of writing to encapsulate his experience. And to prevent being ridiculed or scrutinized, he penned the work under a **pseudonym**.

NEW WORDS

reciprocity
ˌresəˈpräsətē

pseudonym
ˈso͞odn-im

Spartan
ˈspɑːt(ə)n

vignette
vinˈyet

numerous
ˈn(y)o͞om(ə)rəs

Definitions: Try matching the word in the box with the appropriate definition. If you are stuck, check the glossary in the back of the book or the passage at the top of the page.

1.	reciprocity	________	a.	characterized by austerity or lack of comfort or luxury
2.	pseudonym	________	b.	many; abundant; great in number
3.	Spartan	________	c.	a fictitious name, often used by authors
4.	vignette	________	d.	the process of exchanging with others for mutual benefit
5.	numerous	________	e.	a brief, evocative account or description

Sentences: Try to use the words above in a sentence below. Remember that a word ending may be changed or its figure of speech slightly altered.

6. Bethany's short story was a beautiful ____________________ that served as a window into her thoughts, feelings, and soul.
7. Buddhist monks usually live a(n) ____________________ lifestyle: they exist in a(n) world largely devoid of material goods and luxuries.
8. Because the novelist did not want her identity revealed to the public, she created a(n) ____________________ under which she published her romance books.
9. One cannot have a healthy relationship without ____________________: if people do not share, they cannot grow.
10. To my knowledge, there are ____________________ activities to do on a first date; the possibilities seem endless!

Lesson 219

NEW WORDS

asphyxiate
asˈfiksēˌāt

catapult
ˈkatəˌpəlt, -ˌpo͝olt

compelled
kəmˈpel

detritus
diˈtrītəs

predominant
priˈdämənənt

SHERIFF MATT

Compelled by a persistent sense of enforcing justice, Matt decided to become a sheriff. Law enforcement in the small town of Midland was often a mundane task, especially since the **predominant** types of crime in down were misdemeanors and small infractions. But when someone in town **asphyxiated** a six-year-old girl, Matt knew that an important crime needed to be solved. Sifting through the **detritus** and other evidence from the crime scene, Matt eventually surmised that the murderer was a fugitive criminal. When Matt got his colleagues to apprehend the killer and bring him to justice, he **catapulted** from obscurity to fame.

Definitions: Try matching the word in the box with the appropriate definition. If you are stuck, check the glossary in the back of the book or the passage at the top of the page.

1. asphyxiate __________ a. present as the main or most salient element
2. catapult __________ b. waste or debris of any kind
3. compelled __________ c. to kill someone by depriving them of air
4. detritus __________ d. to feel forced or obliged to do something
5. predominant __________ e. (n.) a device that allows one to launch someone or something in a direction; (v.) to launch someone or something in a direction

Sentences: Try to use the words above in a sentence below. Remember that a word ending may be changed or its figure of speech slightly altered.

6. Kelsey felt ____________________ to take Alistair to dinner after she heard that he had been eating alone for two weeks.
7. Even though I like the buildings on campus, the ____________________ reason that I am attending this university is because of its stellar professors.
8. The once clean town now is crumbling and its streets are filled with ____________________ from crumbling infrastructure and waste.
9. After solving an outstanding problem in the field of mathematics, the unknown professor was ____________________ to fame.
10. The murderer placed a garbage bag over his victim in an attempt to ____________________ him, thus ending his life.

Lesson 220

A FICTITIOUS COLONIAL AMERICAN BIOGRAPHY

One could surmise that John Smith led the life of a typical American colonist. In the early seventeenth century, he began the **emigration** process of leaving England and sailing across the Atlantic Ocean to come to America. He arrived on with a contract of **indenture**, which bound him to a cobbler for seven years to train him in the art of shoemaking. But after four years of hard work, John could no longer **brook** his supervisor's guidance, as his mentor was not skilled at his job. Worried that he was being trained by an **imbecile**, John violated his contract and sought employment elsewhere. But most of John's fellow colonists found his personality **grating** and difficult, so John never amounted to anything in his environment.

NEW WORDS

indenture
inˈdenCHər

emigration
ˌemiˈgrāSHən

imbecile
ˈimbəsəl, -ˌsil

brook
bro͝ok

grating
ˈgrātiNG

Definitions: Try matching the word in the box with the appropriate definition. If you are stuck, check the glossary in the back of the book or the passage at the top of the page.

1.	indenture	__________	a.	a formal legal agreement, contract, or document, often tying an apprentice to a master for a fixed term
2.	emigration	__________	b.	a stupid person
3.	imbecile	__________	c.	(n.) a small stream; (v.) to tolerate or allow
4.	brook	__________	d.	sounding harsh and unpleasant; annoying
5.	grating	__________	e.	the process of leaving one's country to settle elsewhere

Sentences: Try to use the words above in a sentence below. Remember that a word ending may be changed or its figure of speech slightly altered.

6. During the latter decades of the nineteenth century there was mass ____________________ from Eastern Europe to the United States.
7. Despite Marylou's high tolerance, it was difficult for her to ____________________ Kyle's manic, suicidal behavior in her class.
8. Only a(n) ____________________ would hand out his or her life savings freely to strangers.
9. Often doctoral students feel like they are living a life of ____________________ because they serve for years under a thesis adviser before becoming professors.
10. It is hard to study with such ____________________ noise coming from the machines outside running incessantly.

Word Search

Lessons 211-220

M D E L L E P M O C G X R Y R
S E R U T N E D N I E K T B S
O W R N U Q I P N R P I Z U L
C M L B L P T N I U C Z O N T
O Q M G P L H U C O O I L L G
R A Y E T N Q E R E R P U T B
C M R Q M N O P A A N P X K P
I Y I B I I I I F V A S B E N
M N N T I C G I T T A F E P Q
A O C A E T T R A A E L L D Y
W D I R D L R C A T C A K T Y
K U S D U V V A T T C O T M J
I E I M W Q E E T E I A V D Y
S S O Y V Y R N B O N O G K W
H P N M Q R J O T M R T N V L

1 to explain and present a theory or idea systematically and in detail
2 sentimental in a feeble or discomforting way
3 to ask information from someone
4 a strong feeling of suitability for a career or occupation; a person's employment or job
5 a harmless pill prescribed for psychological benefit rather than for physiological effect
6 a community, situation, or place regarded as encapsulating key qualities of something larger
7 the arrival of a notable thing, person, or event
8 an independent person or body appointed to settle a dispute
9 to restrain with chains or manacles (literally or metaphorically)
10 smart and fashionable (usually of a person or of clothing)
11 a violent or sudden disruption to something
12 very angry; enraged
13 many and of various different types
14 a surgical cut made into the skin or flesh
15 the process of exchanging with others for mutual benefit
16 a fictitious name, often used by authors
17 (n.) a device that allows one to launch someone or something in a direction; (v.) to launch someone or something in a direction
18 to feel forced or obliged to do something
19 a formal legal agreement, contract, or document, often tying an apprentice to a master for a fixed term
20 the process of leaving one's country to settle elsewhere

Vocabulary Review
Lessons 211-220

Directions: Match each word with its best approximate definition. Note that definitions are not necessarily repeated verbatim from the lesson exercises.

1.	devour	________	a.	a stupid person
2.	aural	________	b.	characterized by austerity; sparing in comfort or luxury
3.	masterful	________	c.	ill-tempered and unfriendly
4.	craving	________	d.	a brief, evocative account of something; a small illustration or portrait photo that fades into the background without an explicit border
5.	simulate	________	e.	lacking in a quality, skill, or ingredient
6.	gaffe	________	f.	a person with much experience in a particular field; a person who has served in the military
7.	veteran	________	g.	to tolerate or allow something
8.	persona	________	h.	powerful enough to control others; done very skillfully
9.	deficient	________	i.	to kill someone by suffocation or depriving them of air
10.	flora	________	j.	to imitate the character or appearance of something
11.	surly	________	k.	comically or repulsively ugly; inappropriate to a shocking degree
12.	profess	________	l.	waste or debris
13.	waft	________	m.	a powerful or insatiable desire for something
14.	grotesque	________	n.	to pass gently or easily through the air
15.	Spartan	________	o.	relating to the ear or a sense of hearing
16.	vignette	________	p.	to eat ravenously and quickly
17.	asphyxiate	________	q.	an unintentional remark or act that causes embarrassment to its originator
18.	detritus	________	r.	to claim openly and often untruthfully that one has a certain feeling or quality
19.	imbecile	________	s.	the plants of a particular region, habitat, or period
20.	brook	________	t.	an aspect of someone's character that is perceived or presented to ve others

Idiomatic Expressions III

This list is a culmination of common idiomatic expressions. It is the final unit in a three-part sequence. Note that these three units are hardly exhaustive of English language idioms.

Idiomatic Expression	Meaning/Example
to know the ropes	To understand the details of a situation or task. Even though it was Vy's first day at Central High, she knew the ropes of how to teach chemistry because she earned a chemistry degree and had taught it before at five schools.
to save face	To avoid humiliation or embarrassment in an attempt to save dignity When Trang was accused of not paying her employees, she quietly paid them but said nothing to them in order to save face.
to strike while the iron is hot	Seize an opportunity while you have the chance. Kendra, whose research on black holes was fascinating, struck while the iron was hot and applied to Harvard when she heard that the astronomy department was seeking a researcher who had expertise in black holes.

Pyrrhic victory	**A victory for someone, but at significant and often detrimental personal cost.** **Shirley succeeded at getting the management fired at her company, but it was a Pyrrhic victory because she hurt her reputation and lost her job in doing so.**
ball is in someone's court	**The decision to act is that of the person whose court the ball is in** **After Uyen told Antonio that she did not want to date him, he told her that the ball was in her court to articulate whether she wanted a friendship with him as a result.**
to tilt at windmills	**To fight against imaginary enemies or to fight a battle that cannot be won** **When Ellen said that she was on the quest to develop a medicine that would allow humans to live to be 10000 years old, her friends told her that her quest for immortality was tilting at windmills.**
to go out on a limb	**To state an opinion or defend a perspective that is very different from other people's** **All of the professors except Mario thought the student was an idiot, but Mario went out on a limb and defended the student's intelligence.**
to put the cart before the horse	**To have things in the wrong order; to have things confused or mixed up.** **Dante put the cart before the horse when he bought movie tickets for his date with Diana before asking her out.**

bitter pill to swallow	An unpleasant fact that has to be accepted It was a bitter pill for Micah to swallow that her cat died in the earthquake and would never again comfort her with its endearing purr.
devil's advocate	To deliberately argue against a position in order to assess the validity of an argument Even though I supported Vu marrying his girlfriend, I played devil's advocate and presented all of the reasons why he might not want to get married to see if a wedding was indeed a good choice for him.
to take/grab the bull by the horns	To take control of a situation and be proactive about it Both Jake and Eric dreamed of being movie stars, but Eric was successful because he grabbed the bull by the horns at every opportunity he could to advance his career.
to have an axe to grind	To have a strong opinion about something and to convince other people that your opinion is correct Sheryl had an axe to grind with the local ice cream store: she told all of its employees that they were rude and that their food was awful; then she attempted to convince all of her friends to boycott the store and its products.
to have cold feet	To have anxiety or reservations about something Even though Stephen was madly in love with Bethany, he had cold feet and cancelled their wedding the day before the actual event.

to feel (a bit) under the weather	**To feel a bit sick** **Mary felt a bit under the weather so she decided not to go to school.**
to take the wind out of one's sails	**To deflate one's ego** **Sam took the wind out of Corli's sails when he showed her that, contrary to her expectation, she was not the best swimmer on the team.**
to upset the apple cart	**To ruin carefully laid plans** **When Justin revealed that Mario was secretly planning to quit his job, he upset the apple cart for Mario, who wanted nobody to know of his plans.**
a cold shower	**A surprisingly chilly or unpleasantly shocking reception or reaction.** **Huy had a cold shower when he received his exam results: after months of studying, his score was uncomfortably low.**
to make ends meet	**To manage so that one's finances are enough for survival.** **Timothy worked three jobs just to make ends meet so that he could support his family.**
to miss the boat	**To have made an error or been wrong** **Peter missed the boat on his algebra test; he made the same mistakes over and over again on each exam question.**
to take under one's wing	**To protect and mentor somebody** **Jay took the talented student under his wing and trained him to become an excellent writer.**

Key Words With Multiple Definitions

Often in intellectual writing and on standardized tests, words are used that bear multiple definitions. Not knowing alternate meanings of such words can interfere with one's comprehension of a text. Below is a chart of some common words that are used in sophisticated writing. Certain commonly-understood definitions are provided as well as some less common definitions. For the latter case, they are used in sentences. Do note that this list is neither exhaustive of words with multiple definitions nor necessarily exhaustive of every definition for each word below.

Word	More Common Definition(s)	Less Common Definition(s) and Sentence Usage
arrest	(n.) the act of seizing someone to take into custody; (v.) to seize (someone) by legal authority and take into custody	(n.) the stoppage or sudden cessation of motion; (v.) to stop or check (progress or a process) Mackenzie's parents sought to **arrest** their daughter's growing obsession with video games by throwing out all of her gaming consoles and limiting her computer use.
base	(n.) the main place where a person works or stays; (v.) to have as the foundation for (something); to use as a point from which something can develop	(adj.) evil; sordid; wicked; dishonest The **base** queen poisoned all of her enemies to ensure that all of her subjects would revere her.
coin	(n.) a flat and usually round piece of metal used as currency	(v.) to invent or devise a new word or phrase The English playwright William Shakespeare (1564-1616) **coined** the phrase "dead as a doornail" in *Henry VI, Part II*.
comb	(n.) a utensil with a row of narrow teeth used for untangling or arranging the hair	(v.) to search carefully and systematically Georgia realized that she would have to **comb** through all of her papers in order to locate the receipt for the television she had purchased last summer.

conviction	(n.) declaration of guilt, sentence, or judgment	(n.) a firmly held belief or opinion My mathematics teacher said with great **conviction** that if students do not do their homework regularly, then they will struggle with the concepts.
founder	(n.) the creator, originator, founding father, or prime mover, or inventor of something	(v.) to sink; to collapse, backfire, or fall through; to trip up After a cannon pierced its hull, the sloop **foundered** and sank in the bay.
gravity	(n.) the force that attracts a body toward the center of the earth	(n.) extreme or alarming importance Though he heard that Jared was injured in a car accident, Bennett did not realize the **gravity** of the matter until he saw Jared in a wheelchair at the hospital.
marshal	(n.) 1. an officer of the highest rank in the armed forces of some countries; 2. a federal or municipal law officer; 3. A head of a police or fire department; 4. an official responsible for supervising public events (e.g. sports events or parades)	(v.) to arrange or assemble (a group of people, especially soldiers) in order The captain began to **marshal** his forces to send relief to the victims of the recent earthquake.
parochial	(adj.) of or relating to a church parish	(adj.) having a limited or narrow outlook or scope Unlike uncle Ned, who is open-minded and liberal, aunt Marge holds a **parochial** worldview and expects everyone to make life choices that are similar to her life choices.
pedestrian	(n.) a person walking along a road or in a developed area	(adj.) lacking inspiration or excitement; dull A date consisting of simply dinner and a movie is an awfully **pedestrian** idea.
plastic	(n.) a synthetic material made from a wide range of polymers that can be molded into shape when soft and then set into rigid form	(adj.) (of a substance or materials) easily shaped or molded The human brain is somewhat **plastic**; when people learn new things or memorize new information, long lasting functional changes in the brain occur.

qualify	(v.) to be entitled to a particular benefit or privilege by fulfilling a necessary condition	(v.) to make (a statement or assertion) less absolute; to add reservations to Although Kyle's mother told him that he could go out partying with his friends, she **qualified** the statement by saying that he could only do so if he finished his homework and research paper first.
sanction	(n.) a threatened penalty for disobeying a law or rule	(v.) to give official permission or approval for (an action) After a much-heated debate, the aldermen **sanctioned** dog walking in all municipal parks.
sound	(n.) vibrations that travel through air (or another medium) that can be heard when they reach one's ear	(adj.) 1. in good condition; not damaged, diseased, or injured; 2. based on reason, judgment, or sense; 3. financially secure It is **unsound** to drive your car home from a party if you are drunk. Martha made a **sound** decision to invest in her education rather than taking all of her hard earned cash to the local casino.
trace	(n.) 1. A mark or object or indication of the existence or passing of something; (v.) 1. to find or discover by investigation; 2. To copy (a drawing, map, or design) by drawing over its lines on a superimposed and partially transparent sheet of paper	(n.) a very small quantity of something, especially one that is too small to be measured accurately Only **traces** of argon can be found in the earth's atmosphere, which is composed primarily of nitrogen and oxygen.

ANSWER KEY

Lesson 171

1. c
2. e
3. b
4. a
5. d
6. manifest
7. flourish
8. oracle
9. veiled
10. dismantled

Lesson 172

1. d
2. e
3. b
4. a
5. c
6. anomalous
7. itinerant
8. pugnacious
9. clemency
10. predation

Lesson 173

1. b
2. c
3. d
4. e
5. a
6. brusque
7. intermittent
8. imposter
9. renew
10. aroma

Lesson 174

1. c
2. a
3. e
4. b
5. d
6. voluptuous
7. hovered
8. catastrophe
9. motif
10. congenial

Lesson 175

1. d
2. b
3. a
4. e
5. c
6. delusion
7. debacle
8. autocrat
9. recluse
10. debris

Lesson 176

1. c
2. d
3. a
4. e
5. b
6. incarnation
7. postulated
8. salutary
9. querulous
10. lugubrious

Lesson 177

1. e
2. a
3. d
4. b
5. c
6. euphoria
7. durable
8. antipathy
9. gratuitous
10. perennial

Lesson 178

1. b
2. d
3. a
4. e
5. c
6. misgivings
7. kinetic
8. hampered
9. embodiment
10. hovel

Lesson 179

1. c
2. e
3. a
4. b
5. d
6. sacrilegious
7. exultation
8. unremitting
9. indeterminate
10. flouted

Lesson 180

1. d
2. c
3. b
4. a
5. e
6. synergy
7. stunted
8. consigned
9. interleaved
10. alacrity

Word Search: Lessons 171-180

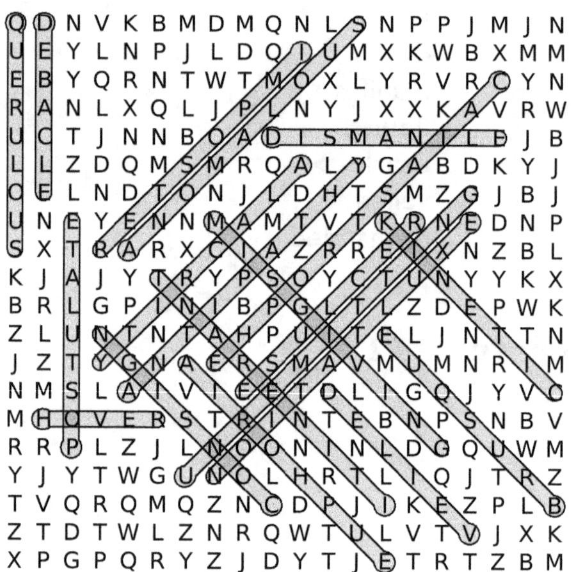

Review: Lessons 171-180

1. e
2. c
3. s
4. a
5. p
6. l
7. m
8. j
9. o
10. t
11. h
12. i
13. r
14. d
15. f
16. q
17. b
18. n
19. g
20. k

Lesson 181

1. c
2. d
3. e
4. b
5. a
6. rancor
7. virtuoso
8. inherent
9. sensationalism
10. precarious

Lesson 182

1. b
2. d
3. e
4. c
5. a
6. remuneration
7. frugal
8. legitimate
9. consternation
10. reproach

Lesson 183

1. b
2. d
3. e
4. a
5. c
6. fraudulent
7. meddle
8. beneficiaries
9. felicity
10. fortitude

Lesson 184

1. c
2. e
3. a
4. b
5. d
6. panacea
7. liberation
8. avuncular
9. thesis
10. exuberant

Lesson 185

1. d
2. e
3. a
4. c
5. b
6. missive
7. unkempt
8. bankruptcy
9. plight
10. aplomb

Lesson 186

1. e
2. d
3. b
4. a
5. c
6. archaic
7. prosperous
8. touted
9. bent
10. derivative

Lesson 187

1. e
2. a
3. b
4. c
5. d
6. purified
7. mediate
8. parameters
9. formulaic
10. savanna

Lesson 188

1. e
2. d
3. b
4. c
5. a
6. feasible
7. deleterious
8. contiguous
9. repealed
10. propensity

Lesson 189

1. c
2. d
3. e
4. b
5. a
6. meager
7. conspire
8. coward
9. somnolent
10. unerring

Lesson 190

1. e
2. d
3. a
4. b
5. c
6. obtuse
7. intuition
8. ersatz
9. nonplussed
10. diligent

Crossword Puzzle: Lessons 181-190

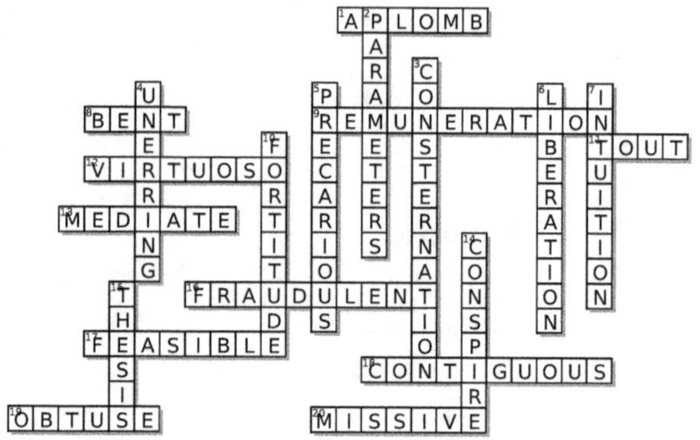

Review: Lessons 181-190

1. a
2. b
3. o
4. c
5. s
6. i
7. g
8. t
9. r
10. m
11. e
12. f
13. k
14. q
15. l
16. d
17. p
18. j
19. h
20. n

Lesson 191

1. e
2. d
3. a
4. b
5. c
6. extract
7. lingering
8. ogled

9. induce
10. thwart

Lesson 192

1. d
2. c
3. a
4. e
5. b
6. jubilant
7. consecrated
8. cognitive
9. impertinence
10. moribund

Lesson 193

1. b
2. d
3. e
4. a
5. c
6. inertia
7. arduous
8. pedagogy
9. engrossing
10. avarice

Lesson 194

1. c
2. e
3. a
4. b
5. d
6. incumbent
7. perpetuates
8. astounds
9. recourse
10. vibrant

Lesson 195

1. c
2. e
3. d
4. b
5. a
6. amenable
7. pundits
8. belabors
9. miscreant
10. unflappable

Lesson 196

1. e
2. d
3. a
4. c
5. b
6. neophyte
7. indolent
8. extinct
9. subordination
10. traversed

Lesson 197

1. c
2. e
3. d
4. a
5. b
6. trepidation
7. disrepute
8. emblem
9. vagary
10. Byzantine

Lesson 198

1. b
2. e
3. a
4. c
5. d

6. elated
7. habituate
8. vitality
9. morbid
10. foundering

Lesson 199

1. e
2. c
3. a
4. d
5. b
6. sparing
7. perseverance
8. astonishing
9. mimicking
10. fragrant

Lesson 200

1. d
2. e
3. b
4. a
5. c
6. leery
7. Becalmed
8. proxy
9. exhaustive
10. severing

Word Search: Lessons 191-200

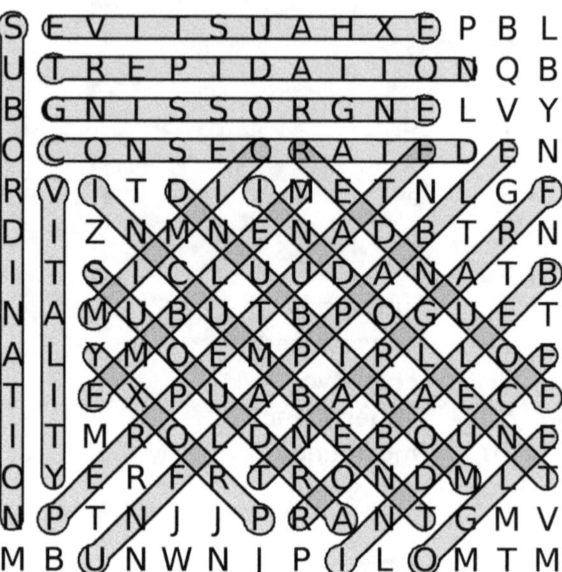

Review: Lessons 191-200

1. m
2. f
3. t
4. p
5. j
6. k
7. c
8. a
9. h
10. r
11. b
12. g
13. o
14. d
15. n
16. i
17. s
18. e
19. q
20. l

Lesson 201

1. b
2. a
3. e
4. d
5. c
6. stickler
7. harangued
8. moderate
9. verbatim
10. guileless

Lesson 202

1. c
2. e
3. d
4. b
5. a
6. arable
7. dilate
8. blissful
9. verbalizing
10. queer

Lesson 203

1. c
2. a
3. d
4. e
5. b
6. blasphemous
7. retrograde
8. impromptu
9. exhorted
10. consonant

Lesson 204

1. c
2. e
3. a
4. b
5. d
6. mystified
7. glutton
8. dismissive
9. distressed
10. proponent

Lesson 205

1. c
2. e
3. a
4. b
5. d
6. serpentine
7. replica
8. unimpeachable
9. imminent
10. fulsome

Lesson 206

1. b
2. a
3. d
4. e
5. c
6. lodging
7. insulate
8. unsolicited
9. gilded
10. immaterial

Lesson 207

1. d
2. c
3. a
4. b
5. e
6. pervades
7. stimulus
8. minutiae
9. Romantic
10. cue

Lesson 208

1. e
2. d
3. a
4. c
5. b
6. prevalent
7. piecemeal
8. crux
9. innuendo
10. relegate

Lesson 209

1. b
2. d
3. e
4. a
5. c
6. ratified
7. taxonomic/taxonomical
8. unbounded
9. prognosis
10. contaminated

Lesson 210

1. e
2. d
3. b
4. c
5. a
6. reprieve
7. inhabited
8. varied
9. uncouth
10. interminable

Crossword Puzzle: Lessons 201-210

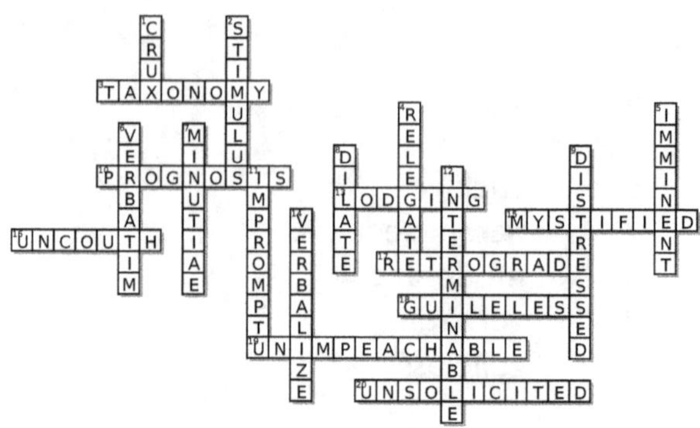

Review: Lessons 201-210

1. l
2. b
3. r
4. j
5. p
6. m
7. f
8. h
9. a
10. t
11. n
12. o
13. g
14. i
15. c
16. q
17. d
18. e
19. s
20. k

Lesson 211

1. c
2. a
3. b
4. e
5. d
6. aural
7. expound
8. recriminations

9. devour
10. mawkish

Lesson 212

1. d
2. a
3. e
4. c
5. b
6. unwitting
7. vocation
8. craving
9. inquire
10. masterful

Lesson 213

1. b
2. a
3. d
4. e
5. c
6. placebos
7. simulate
8. gaffes
9. voluminous
10. microcosm

Lesson 214

1. e
2. d
3. a
4. b
5. c
6. semantic
7. veteran
8. advent
9. arbitrator
10. persona

Lesson 215

1. e
2. d
3. b
4. c
5. a
6. inordinate
7. fetter
8. flora
9. deficient
10. natty

Lesson 216

1. a
2. b
3. c
4. d
5. e
6. surly
7. incensed
8. profess
9. anthropomorphize
10. upheaval

Lesson 217

1. e
2. d
3. b
4. a
5. c
6. authenticate
7. incision
8. multifarious
9. wafting
10. grotesque

Lesson 218

1. d
2. c
3. a
4. e
5. b
6. vignette

7. Spartan
8. pseudonym
9. reciprocity
10. numerous

Lesson 219

1. c
2. e
3. d
4. b
5. a
6. compelled
7. predominant
8. detritus
9. catapulted
10. asphyxiate

Lesson 220

1. a
2. e
3. b
4. c
5. d
6. emigration
7. brook
8. imbecile
9. indenture
10. grating

Word Search: Lessons 211-220

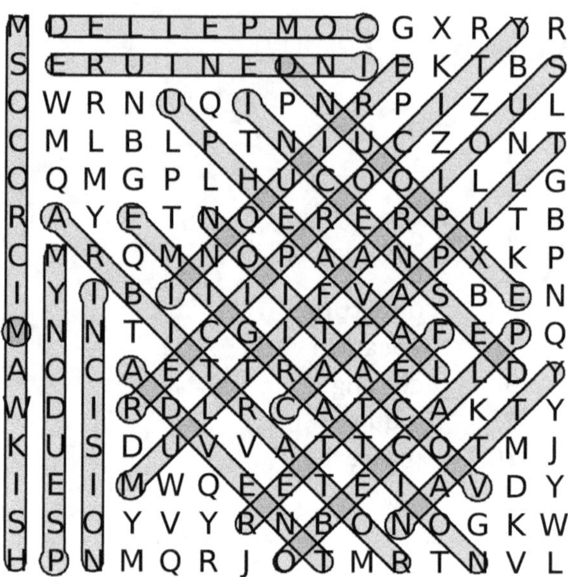

Review: Lessons 211-220

1. p
2. o
3. h
4. m
5. j
6. q
7. f
8. t
9. e
10. s
11. c
12. r
13. n
14. k
15. b
16. d
17. i
18. l
19. a
20. g

GLOSSARY

This glossary contains definitions of the new words from every lesson contained in this book. Please note that not every meaning of each word is contained in this glossary. Generally, only the most commonly used meanings of the words below are defined.

All entries in the glossary take the following form:

word (lesson): (part of speech) definition

Key for parts of speech:
adj. = adjective adv. = adverb n. = noun v. = verb

A

advent (214): (n.) the arrival of a notable thing, person, or event

alacrity (180): (n.) an eagerness or cheerful readiness

amenable (195): (adj.) open and responsive to suggestion

anomalous (172): (adj.) deviating from what is normal or expected

anthropomorphize (216): (v.) to attribute human characteristics to the behavior of an animal, object, or god

antipathy (177): (n.) a strong feeling of dislike

aplomb (185): (n.) confidence and skill shown especially in a difficult situation

arable (202): (adj.) suitable for growing crops

arbitrator (214): (n.) an independent person or body appointed to settle a dispute

archaic (186): (adj.) antiquated; ancient

arduous (193): (adj.) very difficult; challenging

aroma (173): (n.) a distinctive, pleasant smell

asphyxiate (219): (v.) to kill someone by depriving them of air

astonishing (199): (adj.) startling; stunning; amazing

astound (194): (v.) to astonish; to flabbergast; to amaze

aural (211): (adj.) of or related to the ear or sense of hearing

authenticate (217): (v.) to prove or show something to be genuine

autocrat (175): (n.) a ruler who has absolute power

avarice (193): (n.) greed

avuncular (184): (adj.) like an uncle

B

bankrupt (185): (adj.) 1. describing a person or organization unable to pay debts; 2. depleted or impoverished; 3. completely lacking in a particular quality or value; (n.) a person deemed to be insolvent by the court system (v.) to reduce a person or organization to insolvency

becalm (200): (v.) to deprive (a ship) of wind necessary to move it

belabor (195): (v.) to repeat an idea or argument to emphasize it

beneficiaries (183): (n.) people that benefit from something, usually a trust or will

bent (186): (n.) a strong inclination; talent

blasphemous (203): (adj.) sacrilegious; against God or sacred things

bliss (202): (n.) perfect happiness; great joy

brook (220): (n.) a small stream; (v.) to tolerate or allow

brusque (173): (adj.) offhand or abrupt in speech or manner

Byzantine (197): (adj.) labyrinthine; intricate

C

catapult (219): (n.) a device that allows one to launch someone or something in a direction; (v.) to launch someone or something in a direction

catastrophe (174): (n.) a terrible disaster

clemency (172): (n.) lenience or mercy

cognitive (192): (adj.) involving conscious mental activities

compelled (219): (v.) to feel forced or obliged to do something

congenial (174): (adj.) suitable or appropriate; pleasant

consecrated (192): (adj.) dedicated to a sacred purpose

consign (180): (v.) to deliver something to a person's custody; to send (something) to a person to be sold; to assign permanently

consonance (203): (n.) agreement or compatibility between opinions or actions

conspire (189): (v.) to secretly plan to do something harmful or illegal

consternation (182): (n.) a strong feeling of surprise or sudden disappointment that causes confusion

contaminate (209): (v.) to make impure by adding a polluting substance

contiguous (188): (adj.) touching; adjacent

coward (189): (n.) a person who shows a shameful lack of courage

craving (212): (n.) a powerful desire for something

crux (208): (n.) the decisive or most important point at issue

cue (207): (n.) a thing said or done that serves as a signal for action

D

debacle (175): (n.) a complete failure

debris (175): (n.) scattered fragments

deficient (215): (adj.) lacking in a specified ingredient, ability, or quality

deleterious (188): (adj.) damaging or harmful

delusion (175): (n.) a belief that is not true; a false idea

derivative (186): (adj.) made up of parts from something else

detritus (219): (n.) waste or debris of any kind

devour (211): (v.) to eat or read with great intensity and in large quantity

dilate (202): (v.) to make wider or larger; to open

diligent (190): (adj.) painstaking; assiduous

dismantle (171): (v.) to take something apart

dismissive (204): (adj.) feeling that something is unworthy of consideration

disrepute (197): (n.) lack of good reputation

distressed (204): (adj.) suffering from anxiety, sorrow, or pain

durable (177): (adj.) able to withstand wear, pressure or damage

E

elate (198): (v.) to make (someone) extremely happy

emblem (197): (n.) a person or thing that represents an idea

embodiment (178): (n.) someone or something that perfectly represents a certain quality, idea, or feeling

emigration (220): (n.) the process of leaving one's country to settle elsewhere

engrossing (193): (adj.) absorbing all of one's attention and interest

ersatz (190): (adj.) being a usually artificial and inferior substitute

euphoria (177): (n.) intense happiness and excitement

exhaustive (200): (adj.) complete; comprehensive; full-scale

exhort (203): (v.) to urge or encourage one to do something

expound (211): (v.) to present and explain an idea systematically and in detail

extinct (196): (adj.) no longer existing

extract (191): (v.) 1. to remove or take out; 2. to obtain a substance or resource by a special method

exuberant (184): (adj.) filled with energy and enthusiasm

exultation (179): (n.) a feeling of triumphant happiness

F

feasible (188): (adj.) capable of being done, effected

felicity (183): (n.) 1. great happiness; 2. a talent for speaking or writing

fetter (215): (adj.) to restrain with chains or manacles (literally or metaphorically)

flora (215): (n.) the plants of a particular region, habitat, or geological period

flourish (171): (n.) 1.a bold or extravagant gesture; 2. an ornamental flowing curve in writing; (v.) to grow or develop in a healthy or vigorous way

flout (179): (v.) to openly disregard (a rule, law or convention)

formulaic (187): (adj.) produced in accordance with a followed rule or style

fortitude (183): (n.) mental strength in facing adversity

founder (198): (n.) someone who establishes an institution or settlement; (v.) 1. to collapse or fail (of a plan or endeavor); 2. to fill with water and sink (of a ship)

fragrant (199): (adj.) aromatic; perfumed; scented

fraudulent (183): (adj.) cheating; dishonest

frugal (182): (adj.) sparing economically

fulsome (205): (adj.) flattering to an excessive degree

G

gaffe (213): (n.) an unintentional remark or act lavishing embarrassment on its originator; a blunder

gilded (206): (adj.) covered thinly with gold leaf or gold paint

glutton (204): (n.) a person who is usually fond of or eager for something (often food)

grating (220): (adj.) sounding harsh and unpleasant; annoying

gratuitous (177): (adj.) not necessary or appropriate

grotesque (217): (adj.) comically or repulsively ugly; incongruous to a shocking degree

guileless (201): (adj.) innocent and without deception

H

habituate (198): (v.) to make or become accustomed or used to something

hamper (178): (v.) to slow the movement, progress, or action of someone or something

harangue (201): (v.) to lecture at length in an aggressive, critical manner

hovel (178): (n.) a small, squalid, and unpleasant dwelling

hover (174): (v.) to remain in one place in the air

I

imbecile (220): (n.) a stupid person

immaterial (206): (adj.) unimportant under the circumstances; irrelevant

imminent (205): (adj.) about to happen

impertinence (192): (n.) irrelevance, inappropriateness, or absurdity

imposter (173): (n.) a person who deceives others by pretending to be someone else

impromptu (203): (adj. and adv.) done without being planned, organized, or rehearsed

incarnation (176): (n.) a person who represents a quality or idea

incensed (216): (adj.) very angry; enraged

incision (217): (n.) a surgical cut made into the skin or flesh

incumbent (194): (n.) someone currently holding office

indenture (220): (n.) a formal legal agreement, contract, or document, often tying an apprentice to a master for a fixed term

indeterminate (179): (adj.) not exactly known, defined, or established

indolent (196): (adj.) lazy

induce (191): (v.) to cause someone to do something

inertia (193): (n.) 1. a tendency to do nothing or remain unchanged; resistance to change in some physical property; 2. (in physics) a property where an object remains in its existing rest state or in straight line motion unless acted upon by an external force

inhabit (210): (v.) to live in or occupy a place or environment

inherent (181): (adj.) innate; native; inbred

innuendo (208): (n.) a suggestive, allusive, often disparaging remark

inordinate (215): (adj.) unusually or disproportionally large; excessive

inquire (212): (v.) to ask information from someone

insulate (206): (v.) to use a material to protect something from the elements or heat loss

interleave (180): (v.) to insert pages between other pages; to put something in between the layers of

interminable (210): (adj.) unending; unceasing

intermittent (173): (adj.) occurring at irregular intervals

intuition (190): (n.) quick and ready insight; the ability to know something without having proof

itinerant (172): (adj.) traveling from place to place

J

jubilant (192): (adj.) rejoicing; triumphant; joyous

K

kinetic (178): (adj.) of, resulting from, or pertaining to motion

L

leery (200): (adj.) suspicious; wary

legitimate (182): (adj.) legal; valid; sanctioned

liberation (184): (n.) the act of freeing someone from slavery, imprisonment or oppression; a release

lingering (191): (adj.) staying beyond expected time

lodging (206): (n.) a place where someone lives or stays temporarily

lugubrious (176): (adj.) full of sadness or sorrow

M

manifest (171): (n.) a customs document listing the people and contents of a ship, train, or plane; (v.) 1. to show or demonstrate clearly; 2. to be evidence of, to prove; 3. (of a ghost or an illness) to appear

masterful (212): (adj.) powerful and able to control others; performed or performing extremely skillfully

mawkish (211): (adj.) sentimental in a feeble or discomforting way

meager (189): (adj.) deficient in quantity or quality

meddle (183): (v.) to be involved in activities of other people, especially when they do not want your involvement

mediate (187): (v.) to intervene between people in a dispute in order to bring about a resolution or agreement

microcosm (213): (n.) a community, situation, or place regarded as encapsulating key qualities of something larger

mimic (199): (v.) to imitate; to copy

minutiae (207): (n.) small, precise, or trivial details of something

miscreant (195): (n.) a person who behaves badly or in a way that breaks the law

misgiving (178): (n.) a feeling of doubt or anxiety about the consequences or outcome of something

missive (185): (n.) a written message; letter

moderate (201): (adj.) 1. average in amount, intensity, or degree; 2. not politically radical; (n.) a person who does not hold radical views; (v.) 1. to make less extreme, intense or violent; 2. to preside over

morbid (198): (adj.) cheerless; unpleasant; morose

moribund (192): (adj.) no longer active or effective; very sick; close to death

motif (174): (n.) a theme that is repeated through a book, story, etc.; a decorative pattern

multifarious (217): (adj.) many and of various different types

mystified (204): (adj.) (for someone) to be utterly bewildered or perplexed

N

natty (215): (adj.) smart and fashionable (usually of a person or of clothing)

neophyte (196): (n.) a beginner, greenhorn, tyro

nonplussed (190): (adj.) utterly perplexed

numerous (218): (adj.) many; abundant; great in number

O

obtuse (190): (adj.) stupid or unintelligent

ogle (191): (v.) to stare at in a manner showing sexual desire

oracle (171): (n.) a person with great wisdom; someone believed to communicate with a deity

P

panacea (184): (n.) a remedy for all disease; a solution for all problems

parameters (187): (n.) guidelines that control what something is or how something should be done

pedagogy (193): (n.) the art, science, or profession of teaching

perennial (177): (adj.) 1. existing or continuing in the same way for a long time; 2. (of people) appearing permanently engaged in a specified way of life; 3. (of plants) living for several years

perpetuate (194): (v.) 1. to make something continue indefinitely; 2. to preserve something valued from oblivion or extinction

perseverance (199): (n.) determination; endurance

persona (214): (n.) the aspect of one's character presented to or perceived by others

pervade (207): (v.) to spread through and be perceived in all parts of a place

piecemeal (208): (adj.) characterized by unsystematic partial measures taken over a period of time

placebo (213): (n.) a harmless pill prescribed for psychological benefit rather than for physiological effect

plight (185): (n.) a dangerous, unfortunate, or difficult situation

postulate (176): (n.) a thing assumed to be true as the basis for reasoning; (v.) to assume the truth or basis of something for the basis of reasoning or belief

precarious (181): (adj.) unstable, unsure; uncertain; dubious

predation (172): (n.) the act of preying on other animals; attacking or plundering

predominant (219): (adj.) present as the main or most salient element

prevalent (208): (adj.) widespread in a particular area at a particular time

profess (216): (v.) to claim openly (and often falsely) that one possesses a certain feeling or quality

prognosis (209): (n.) forecasted outcome of a situation or disease

propensity (188): (n) a strong natural tendency to do something

proponent (204): (n.) a person who advocates a project, cause, or theory

prosperous (186): (adj.) flourishing; successful; thriving

proxy (200): (n.) the authority to represent someone else, especially in voting

pseudonym (218): (n.) a fictitious name, often used by authors

pugnacious (172): (adj.) eager or quick to argue or fight

pundit (195): (n.) an expert who usually gives speeches in public

purify (187): (v.) to make unadulterated or clear; to free from guilt or dirt

Q

queer (202): (adj.) strange; odd

querulous (176): (adj.) complaining in an annoyed way

R

rancor (181): (n.) anger or dislike for someone

ratify (209): (v.) to sign or give formal consent to a contract, treaty, or agreement to make it formally valid

reciprocity (218): (n.) the process of exchanging with others for mutual benefit

recluse (175): (n.) one who lives a solitary existence and who often avoids people

recourse (194): (n.) an opportunity or choice to use or do something in order to deal with a problem or situation

recriminations (211): (n.) an accusation in response to one from someone else

relegate (208): (v.) to consign to an inferior mark or position

remuneration (182): (n.) compensation; pay for a service

renew (173): (v.) to make new, fresh, or strong again

repeal (188): (v.) to revoke or annul (a vote or congressional act)

replica (205): (n.) an exact model of something

reprieve (210): (n.) a cancellation or postponement of punishment; (v.) to cancel or postpone the punishment of someone

reproach (182): (n.) rebuke; disapproval; discredit

retrograde (203): (adj.) directed or moving backwards; reversed

romanticism (207): (n.) the state or quality of expressing feelings, inspiration, and subjectivity over reason

S

sacrilege (179): (n.) a violation or misuse of what is regarded as holy or sacred

salutary (176): (adj.) having a good or helpful result (especially after something unpleasant has happened)

savanna (187): (n.) a grassy plain with few trees usually found in tropical or subtropical areas

semantic (214): (adj.) related to meaning in logic or language

sensationalism (181): (n.) the use of shocking details to cause excitement

serpentine (205): (adj.) winding or twisting

sever (200): (v.) 1. to divide by cutting or slicing; 2. to terminate or break off a connection or relationship

simulate (213): (v.) to imitate the character or appearance of

somnolent (189): (adj.) likely to induce sleep

sparing (199): (adj.) economical; frugal; meager

Spartan (218): (adj.) characterized by austerity or lack of comfort or luxury

stickler (201): (n.) a person who demands a certain quality or type of behavior

stimulus (207): (n.) 1. a signal or event that evokes a reaction by a tissue or organ; 2. a thing that rouses activity in someone or something; 3. an exciting or interesting quality

stunted (180): (adj.) someone or something whose growth, development, or progress is or has been hindered

subordination (196): (n.) the act of placing in a lower rank or position

surly (216): (adj.) bad-tempered and unfriendly

synergy (180): (n.) increased effectiveness resulting from combined action

T

taxonomy (209): (n.) branch of science dealing with the classification of organisms; the classification of something; a scheme of classification

thesis (184): (n.) a statement that someone wants to discuss or prove

thwart (191): (v.) to frustrate or baffle; to oppose

tout (186): (v.) to persuade; to promote; to talk up

traverse (196): (v.) to cross; to cut across

trepidation (197): (n.) feeling of fear that something may happen

U

unbounded (209): (adj.) limitless

uncouth (210): (adj.) lacking good manners, refinement, or grace

unerring (189): (adj.) always right or accurate

unflappable (195): (adj.) imperturbable; to be able to remain calm in a difficult situations

unimpeachable (205): (adj.) unable to be doubted or questioned; entirely trustworthy

unkempt (185): (adj.) having an untidy or disheveled appearance

unremitting (179): (adj.) never stopping or lessening

unsolicited (206): (adj.) not requested; done voluntarily

unwitting (212): (adj.) a person not aware of the full facts; not done purposefully

upheaval (216): (n.) a violent or sudden disruption to something

V

vagary (197): (n.) whim; unusual idea

varied (210): (adj.) showing a number of different types of elements

veiled (171): (adj.) covered or concealed

verbalize (202): (v.) to express ideas or feelings in words, often by speaking out loud

verbatim (201): (adj. and adv.) in exactly the same words as used originally

veteran (214): (n.) 1. a person experienced in a particular field; 2. a person who has served in the military

vibrant (194): (adj.) showing great life, activity, and energy; very bright and strong

vignette (218): (n.) a brief, evocative account or description

virtuoso (181): (n.) one who excels in something especially art, or music

vitality (198): (n.) vigorousness; exuberance

vocation (212): (n.) a strong feeling of suitability for a career or occupation; a person's employment or job

voluminous (213): (adj.) large in volume; occupying much space

voluptuous (174): (adj.) suggesting sensual pleasure by fullness and beauty of form

W

waft (217): (v.) to pass or cause gently to pass through the air

www.ingramcontent.com/pod-product-compliance
Lightning Source LLC
LaVergne TN
LVHW081633120826
845149LV00025B/1903

* 9 7 8 0 9 9 8 4 8 4 1 4 3 *